MW00353215

Amazing Heights

How Short Guys Stand Tall

By

Seth Ulinski

Copyright © 2018 by Seth Ulinski

All rights reserved

Table of Contents

Preface

I've always appreciated the *underdog* – a person or a team facing adversity or challenging odds for success. As a kid, I would root for athletes considered to be short or undersized compared to larger opponents. As an adult, I noted that short men could similarly take on the underdog label given the emphasis society places on height. Although I knew the reasons in part, as a short guy I still I wondered why society favors taller guys.

Outside of sports, obstacles for short males come in two forms. The first is society's *height bias* – the belief that taller people are better (spoiler alert: this is what is referred to as a false cognitive bias). The second and typically larger obstacle comes in the form of *self-limiting beliefs (yes, we can be our own worst enemies)*. In the age of social media and digital profiles, we are increasingly measured, compared and judged. Bullies and naysayers are everywhere. False cognitive biases and height discrimination run rampant. As I continued my quest for personal development, I thought *wouldn't it be great if there was content to address the specific challenges for short guys.* I found a few resources but nothing comprehensive.

This book educates, motivates and provides action items for the short guy fraternity. It examines height data from different professions (not just sports) and discusses research from experts in genetics and behavioral psychology. It seeks to motivate readers by sharing uplifting stories of short men who've accomplished amazing heights in life. In addition to these U.S. heroes, global media icons, and high-flying entrepreneurs. It discusses research in genetics and behavioral psychology. It provides action items in fashion, health, and dating. There are anecdotes from my travels and experiences to keep things real and relatable while adding a dash of comic relief.

The book's content largely focuses on the individual, rather than society. It encourages the reader to be open to new ways of thinking and to take responsibility for their actions, providing tools to help them along the way.

Acknowledgements

I would like to thank my mom for showing me that even small and soft-spoken people can be world-class athletes who inspire others. I would like to thank my dad for giving me an appreciation for sports and the outdoors. I would like to thank my sister, Britt, for believing in me and always referring to me as "big bro." You've each helped me become the person I am today.

I would like to thank my editors, JoAnne Dyer and Stacy Bingham, for fusing my quirky ideas and writing style into a cohesive book (I promise to take credit for all unnecessary hyphens and parentheses). I would like to thank Erika Stokes for her book formatting prowess.

I would like to thank Lewis Agrell for the eye-catching cover design. I would also like to thank Justin Merrill for his creative wizardry.

I would like to thank the following people who shared experiences, read early drafts, or helped in other ways:

Scott Crockett, Izzet Agoren, Dennis Duquette, Bob Northrup, Jeff Greenfield, Derrick Kosinski, Rob Daliege, Glenn Grasso, Brian Chamberlain, Andrea Beatty, Tanya Osensky, Richard Evensen, Heather Taylor, Leslie Donahue, Darayl Remick, Ron Caddick, Zachary Hanby, John Hunter, Chris Long, Paul Ash and Lisa Currie.

As knowledge is power, I would like to thank the following publications and podcasts for powering up my book:

Authority Self-Publishing, Entrepreneurs On Fire, The Tim Ferriss Show, The Modest Man, Operation Self Reset *and* The Distilled Man.

I would like to thank the doctors, therapists and other staff who've allowed me to continue doing the activities I love, including Dr. Charles Blitzer, Dr. Robert Zeits, Dr. Erica Brown, Claude Hillel, and Matt Donahue. Without your work, I wouldn't be standing tall or reaching amazing heights.

Chapter-1

Introduction

Have you been pushed aside, rejected, made fun of, or simply ignored due to your height? In the United States, the average adult male is 5'10". If you fall below this metric, you may face some of these challenges, having been labeled "short" by society. Research confirms what you may already know: society favors taller guys. Height bias in American society is widespread. In general, being taller opens the door for more opportunities in business, politics, dating, and sports. As a result, some guys and teens who are vertically challenged succumb to a defeatist or victim mindset. Who can blame them? After all, society is programmed to think and feel a certain way, which can make life an uphill battle for the not-so-tall.

What is height bias?

What exactly is height bias and why does it exist? In a nutshell, the brain is wired to interpret height as a proxy for social status, which includes health, wealth, and power. Society isn't necessarily being evil with its height bias. Our brains are like computers. They come preprogrammed with software that helps us make quick decisions, shortcuts known as *heuristics*[1] in the world of psychology. Heuristics are valuable in fight or flight situations when we don't have time to think rationally, such as when we're in survival mode. Pause too long when you're facing danger and you may become lunch for a predator. This plays into Darwin's survival of the fittest evolutionary theory. Taller guys are perceived to be stronger and more powerful. This makes them attractive for mating purposes, as well as for positions of leadership. All other things being equal, this bias is why the vertically gifted tend to get the nod over the vertically challenged.

It seems these shortcuts that speed up decision-making and save energy also create *false cognitive biases.* Plenty of guys under 5'10" have become excellent leaders, attained powerful positions, or dominated their professions, and if not you're not aware of any of these guys, keep reading.

Terms used to describe short people

There are many colorful ways to describe being below average in height. Many of these terms don't carry positive connotations and are even derogatory: little guy, shrimp, Smurf, or dwarf (for the record, dwarf is inaccurate if you exceed 4'10"). *Vertically challenged* is a euphemism that has gained acceptance. At 5'7", I'm a member of this fraternity.

6

The short guy fraternity

You may be curious about how many vertically challenged guys are out there. Per the latest U.S. Census data, approximately 60 million adult males qualify for this brotherhood. If you are frustrated and looking for answers, you're not alone. Like many fraternities or brotherhoods, the vertically challenged brotherhood can bond us through shared trials and challenges on the road to initiation. As I researched height bias, it became clear to me that guys under 5'10" shared many of the same experiences. I felt like this created a bond, and at a certain level, we belonged to the same fraternity. However, just like in traditional college fraternities, vertically challenged fraternity members will have different educations, family backgrounds, and belief systems. These differences make us unique. They can provide the launch pad to do amazing things—or if we allow them to, they can limit us.

Plenty of guys are more vertically challenged than I am. Indeed, I am tall for a short guy, if that makes sense. In the U.S., I am taller than about 25 percent of the adult male population. As one of my not so politically correct six-foot buddies so eloquently put it, I'm the "tallest midget."

Midget actually isn't the term used today. *Little people* or *dwarf* are actually the correct terms for the medical or genetic condition that usually results in an adult height of 4'10" or shorter. While I am not a dwarf, I've still faced my fair share of vertical challenges in life, such as when I've competed in sports, searched for clothes that fit properly, worked my way up the corporate ladder, and sought the attention of females.

Height bias needs more research

At first, I thought I was either overly sensitive or too analytical regarding height (if you know me, you know that both are highly possible). However, the more research I conducted and shared, the more validation I received from vertically challenged buddies, female friends, business associates, and from reading biographies and watching documentaries. Height bias—or in extreme cases, *height discrimination,* also referred to as heightism—needed to be explored. There are plenty of articles and clinical studies on height but few are geared towards personal development.

I found books and movies about smaller guys doing big things in sports, and yes, a solid chunk of this book does review the accomplishments of vertically challenged athletes. However, I couldn't find books dedicated to showcasing other professions or career paths for guys who may be facing the height headwinds. And height isn't exactly a key topic in history or business classes.

Time to beat the bias

The final confirmation I needed to embark on this book was a posting[12] by a high school kid who was distraught about being 5'6". At only seventeen years old, this kid was *convinced* he couldn't play sports and would never hold leadership positions—all based on a few articles he'd read. My immediate thought was, *hey this kid is only seventeen and he could still grow a couple inches, maybe more.* Then I wondered what the heck type of message his parents, teachers, and coaches were delivering to him. Unfortunately, he is not alone. If height bias is bad, heightism is evil. If we can agree that racism and sexism are forms of discrimination which shouldn't be tolerated, then why should heightism get swept under the rug? There are frequent reports of short children and teenagers being bullied. In some cases, it is so intense that the victims commit suicide. This is one reason why treatments such as bone-lengthening surgery and human growth hormone (HGH) are becoming more common, despite the risks associated with each.

While height bias may have strong grips in certain areas of life and with some people, our heart and determination cannot be measured. As we review the accolades and achievements of guys in our

---

[1] https://talk.collegeconfidential.com/parent-cafe/1261074-growing-taller.html

fraternity, we find height bias is or was a major challenge for them many times. Other times, it was the least of their challenges.

What can you find in this book?

In this book, I synthesize height data across different professions and compile stories of vertically challenged fraternity members who've achieved amazing heights in life. In addition to being a member of the club, my credentials include a background in market research, a quest for self-improvement, and experience living in small cities like my hometown of Dover, New Hampshire, as well as big cities such as New York, Los Angeles and Boston. I've also faced challenges in the form of a car accident that required reconstructive surgery, leaving me unable to walk for six months, plus thyroid and eye diseases which presented additional character builders.

If you're looking for education, motivation, or strategies, think of this book as a tool to help level the playing field, or at least, to better understand it.

Helping you change your perspective and your life

The goal of this book is to empower vertically challenged guys and their entourage (e.g. parents, coaches, and teachers) with a fresh perspective to help understand and overcome some of the real or self-imposed limitations of height. Whether you identify as a student, athlete, educator, business professional, entertainer, or a combination of these, a shift in your perspective can be life-changing. I am confident the content here will provide at least one takeaway that will enlighten, motivate, or inspire you. In addition to education, this book contains action items. Knowledge is power but as we'll see, action is ultimately where the magic happens. The vertically challenged can adopt a can-do attitude and chart their respective courses in life in spite of the biases they encounter. These action-takers do not allow head-to-toe measurements to dictate the heights they achieve in life. Wouldn't it be a confidence boost to know fourteen U.S. presidents have been under 5'10" and that our fourth president was only 5'4"? How about the fact that NASA sent a 5'5" astronaut into space not once but twice? Are you aware that one of the most iconic figures who fought for equal rights and freedom would be deemed vertically challenged by today's standards? How about the fact that today's digital world is largely architected by guys who are below average in height? Perhaps this book will help pave the way for the next wave of business and creative geniuses to launch their ideas and dreams.

Self-assured short men provide inspiration

Knowing that others of similar stature have done amazing things in the past or are currently rising to the top may ignite an inner fire to help you overcome a hurdle or break free of limiting beliefs, like those of the high school kid I mentioned above. Perhaps reassessing your core values and what's really important to you will help you identify a new path or create new habits. Or maybe one or two life hacks I'll share will be sufficient in helping you become more confident.

Height cannot prevent you from being a good student, an awesome brother, a loving dad, a respected teacher, a pillar of the community, an entrepreneur, a doctor, or a world explorer. An undersized kid may not be tall enough to get on the rollercoaster ride, but he can climb Mt. Kilimanjaro if he sets his mind to it. You are dealt a certain hand when it comes to height. It's up to you to determine how you play your hand.

Changing habits and perspective to deal with height bias

Understanding height bias is one thing. How you deal with the bias is another. I've learned to appreciate and maximize what I have. When I divulge my 5'7" status to people, many times the response is "You don't seem that short." Yes, I could chalk this up to being closer to 5'7½", but kidding aside, I believe my not-so-short appearance can be attributed to a few things, including relatively good posture, a healthy lifestyle, attire that fits, and last but not least, self-confidence. I make an effort to manage each of these areas and am convinced the last item in the list is the result of managing the previous ones. Sometimes things happen which are out of your control, testing you mentally and physically. Control what you can. Start with yourself.

Transitioning from old habits to new ways of thinking and behavior requires regularly doing things differently. I like the motto of becoming comfortable with the uncomfortable. Test and learn. Be bold, be brave. Keep an open mind. Being open to new ideas and ways of thinking can be just as challenging as a new exercise. After all, the same heuristics at work in society are embedded in you.

So let's begin this quest for growth and achieving amazing heights, shall we? Start by standing up with the shoulders back, tuck the chin and squeeze the shoulder blades back and downward. Now place your hands on your hips. If an illustration is helpful, check out the middle guy on the book cover. Per research by psychologist Amy Cuddy, standing tall like this for two minutes increases testosterone levels while decreasing cortisol or stress levels. A valuable exercise just before an interview, public speaking, or any other feat that requires an added dose of courage. In addition to appearing more confident, good posture can add up to two inches to your height.[3]

Chapter-2

Height 101

What determines our height? Can we do anything about it? What is this Napoleonic complex thing that people reference?

These are questions I've pondered at different points in life. As an adult, I thought I knew all the answers. I was wrong. And in case the *"all I know is I know nothing"* quote comes to mind, these are actually Plato's words synthesizing a passage from Socrates, not Socrates himself. OK, I guess that counts as a lesson in English literature. But let's continue.

What factors determine height? As it turns out, the answer, like many things in life, is a bit squishy. Before I started this research, I'd figured height was nearly 100 percent based on genetics. However, there are multiple forces at play. My mom is 5'3" and my dad is 5'10"; however, these numbers are both self-reported, and while I don't believe Mom stretched the tale of the tape (short women tend to face less scrutiny than short men), I always wondered if Dad was really that much taller than I am. Considering my own stretching of the truth, plus other research, I figured there was a good chance Daddio had been adding a couple inches. As fate would have it, he may have been telling me the truth years ago … but Father Time was doing his part.

People "shrink" as we age.[4] This is due to discs between the vertebrae in the spine dehydrating and compressing. The process begins around age fifty for men and women. We can lose up to three inches in height by the time we are eighty years old. While genetics play an important role in this process, protecting bones and muscle can help fight it. Smokers and heavy drinkers are at increased risk of shrinkage, while a healthy diet that includes calcium and vitamin D is beneficial. In case you want another reason to stay active, studies indicate exercise and weight-training also help combat the shrinkage.

Going back to my dad, he recently had spinal fusion surgery. This coupled with being seventy years old means he's likely lost two to three inches of height. With this in mind, I take it back, Dad. You were probably shooting straight about your height. One of the few to be so honest—very admirable. He's an active, healthy guy in general. However, given what I know about vertebrae and spine health, perhaps I should have been more aggressive in recruiting him for yoga and weight-training with me ten years ago. Would it have helped him dodge the knife? Who knows? I am happy that he's made a habit of stretching and posture exercises. I consider this a win.

OK, getting back to height studies and average human height worldwide, per Wikipedia:[5]

"Some studies may allow subjects to self-report values. Generally speaking, self-reported height tends to be taller than measured height, although the overestimation of height depends on the reporting subject's height, age, gender and region."

While Wikipedia may not be a bulletproof resource for facts, how does your driver's license or online dating profile compare to the height during your most recent doctor's visit? If you're like me, there is likely a discrepancy. These are signals that height bias is alive and well in society. Otherwise, why would people want to exaggerate height? Maybe you are in the minority and telling the truth about your height. If so, thank you! Know that you're already doing your part to set an example for the fraternity.

Let's get into the science of what factors into the height of humans. If you think it's almost entirely based on genetics, you'd be wrong. There's more to it. My work in research requires that I firm up beliefs, hunches, and my Spidey sense—with data. In this case, I looked for studies to back up the notion that our height is largely based on heredity, i.e. our parents and their parents.

Molecular biologist Dr. Chao-Quiang Lai of Tufts University shares his research.[6] For starters, Dr. Lai reframes our question:

"How much variation (difference between individuals) in height is attributable to genetic effects and how much to nutritional effects?"

His estimates that 60 to 80 percent of the difference in height between individuals is determined by genetic factors, whereas 20 to 40 percent can be attributed to environmental effects, mainly nutrition. These ranges are based on estimates of the heritability of human height. For statistics enthusiasts, this refers to the proportion of the total variation in height due to genetic factors. Dr. Lai's work also states that ethnic backgrounds also play a role.

So, the height of mom and dad have a significant impact on our height. If they are both above-average in height, it's more likely you will be. My next question: how about the nutrition component? Dr. Lai's work concludes that protein is the most important nutrient when it comes to height. Digging deeper, the study identifies certain minerals, such as calcium, as well as vitamins A and D, influence height. The overarching theme is that malnutrition during childhood, especially teenage years, can be detrimental to height.

My takeaway and full disclosure: I'm not a nutritionist, but I consider myself a student of the healthy eating game and view food as fuel. While my diet won't impact my height, I eat foods with vitamins and minerals: milk, cheese, carrots, and spinach for vitamins A and D, plus chicken, beef, or fish for protein. I'm also a fan of protein powders that provide on-demand protein plus other nutrients. There are even vegetable-based protein powders for non-meat eaters. I'm a fan of a company called Orgain that makes an organic plant protein. Who knew peas could pack such a protein punch? Throughout the years I've also used a combination of whey, a fast-absorbing protein, and casein, a slower-burning protein. If you're not a fan of powders, the company Clif Bar makes a quality protein bar.

The findings from Dr. Lai made me wonder about the purported massiveness of the Vikings, which included my understanding that guys from Denmark were gifted with height. If you're up for a little history lesson, follow along.

During the Viking age (800-1066),[7] the men were typically cast as taller and stronger people. What was their secret? And were the Norsemen hailing from Northern Europe—mainly Denmark, Norway and Sweden—really that much taller than their neighbors? I found limited research on this; however, some findings[8] indicate Vikings were an inch and a half taller than others in the region. While the Vikings didn't have access to ridiculously more or better food sources than their counterparts did, historians agree that their diets included fish, which is high in protein. This could have played a role in the Vikings' height, considering those in present-day Germany and surrounding areas did not have the same access.

The Vikings may have been slightly taller as a result of consuming higher-protein foods. If we look at the Scandinavian[9] region today, the typical man from Denmark is 5'11½" to 6' tall,

Norway 5'11", and Sweden 5'11½". Men from these countries rank as the tallest in the world. I think this gives merit to diet and the hereditary factors.

If you are a young man who is still in growth mode and your family doesn't hail from these fish-filled regions (or even if they do), I'm going out on a limb to say that quality food intake, particularly quality proteins, makes sense. Even if protein doesn't directly promote height, there is plenty of research to support the health benefits of protein.

How about Short Man Syndrome, also known as a Napoleon Complex? Is this a real thing or simply a myth created by taller guys who secretly fear world domination by the vertically challenged?

Psychologist Stanley C. Loewen[10] explains this idea is an informal term and not a medical or psychological condition. Short Man Syndrome is a form of inferiority complex in which the person attempts to overcompensate for their perceived shortcoming. Remember, the key term here, guys, is perceived. It's up to you to decide how much your height affects your life. Control what you can, such as attitude, diet, exercise and environment. Focus on your strengths, interests, and passion points. Surround yourself with positive people.

Loewen explains the stereotype in detail as a *"smaller male with short man syndrome, is aggressive, a loudmouth attention seeker, looking to one-up people and prove themselves, even if it means risky behavior. Many people compare the typical short man complex to that of a smaller dog — which many note are often noisier and more aggressive than larger more docile dogs."* Guys, this shouldn't be confused with the aforementioned quote from Mark Twain which emphasizes the fact we should be more focused on the size of the fight in the dog, not the size of the dog in the fight.

As Loewen continues, he explains the term *Napoleon Complex* refers to Napoleon Bonaparte, who many believed conducted his tyranny and invasions as a form of overcompensation for his short stature. For the record, Napoleon was 5'6", and at the time, this was considered average height.

This article cites research from Ohio University whereby psychologists suggest that larger combatants delay actual combat as much as possible in the hope that the smaller party will recognize the odds are stacked against them and back down. Think David and Goliath, although if you know details of the story, the slower and visually impaired Goliath never had a chance against the smaller, more agile David. While the smaller individual might stand to gain from the confrontation, the larger person is likely already in a strong position. Smaller individuals also require fewer resources and are less hindered by injury due to their smaller body weight. Thus it might not be that smaller males are more prone to attack first or act noisily, but rather "gentle giant syndrome" might cause larger individuals to be more reluctant to engage in confrontation, and the smaller individuals then look more aggressive as a result.

Loewen does examine some positive benefits of being shorter, which can be leveraged to help you gain confidence and overcome Short Man Syndrome (SMS) if you have it, which I imagine many of us do to some extent. For instance, shorter people tend to gain muscle more easily and thus often appear stockier and more imposing despite what they lack in height. Smaller individuals also have a lower center of gravity, which provides a superior combination of balance and agility. A few benefits of being, as Loewen puts it, a *dark horse.*

For smaller guys looking for benefits: how 'bout those apples? This is a *Good Will Hunting* reference, and although a few sources list Matt Damon as 5'10", let's assume society's height bias has gripped even Mr. Damon. If you're not familiar with the movie, you can flex and point at your biceps (an apple) in front of the mirror (hey, you've gotten this far, so let's have fun with this). While I appreciate Loewen's use of the "dark horse" label, I prefer the term underdog. In addition to being a commonly used term in sports, "underdog" resonates with me especially because it brings back memories of the superhero cartoon character I loved as a kid.

For those who aren't familiar with Underdog the cartoon star, try the Google machine or simply envision a nerdly Clark Kent-like dog, who transforms into a dog with Superman-like powers when the call goes out to save the day.

Here's another inspirational quote from Loewen to fuel your athletic *and* dating fires:

"Shorter individuals are also often more agile and have better reflexes and some women prefer shorter men as they are less intimidating or 'cuter'."

A nice two-for-one quote, eh? Of course I am biased here, but having played sports and seen plenty of shiftiness and ankle-breaking moves from shorter guys, I concur. And yes, cuteness can be just as attractive as brute-ness.

Loewen mentions a life hack to gaining height, such as shoe inserts. I initially frowned upon these as I thought they were silly and could also be considered false advertising. However, shoe inserts are relatively inexpensive and easy to use. Plus, my own curiosity and research for this book required that I experiment. Consider me your guinea pig. Yes, I purchased inserts, and you can read my findings in Chapter 17.

You may wonder at times if what you're experiencing really is height bias, or something else. But at times, the discrimination can be very real. As an adult, I've found that these headwinds of discrimination have dwindled for me, but they do pop up from time to time. Ultimately, though, beliefs can be addressed or overcome by taking action mentally or physically. I'm an active guy and tend to favor "doing" in order to confirm or disprove things in everyday life. In this vein, let's consider the following quote from Bruce Lee:

"If you spend too much time thinking about a thing, you'll never get it done."

~ **Bruce Lee**

Thank you, Bruce. OK, let's review, shall we? Science tells us that height is largely determined by genetics, while nutrition tends to be the second largest driver. If you're digging deeper into food and diet for something you can control, though, it may be worth exploring whether you're getting the proper levels of protein in addition to those greens that Mom and Dad harp on.

Also, if anyone ever drops the Napoleon Complex label on you, you can seek refuge in knowing he was a military genius who dominated a massive part of Europe for a decade. Historians will back me up here. Further, Napoleon was average height for the time. And whether you are a fan of tyrants like Napoleon or not, he was decisive—and typically victorious—once he made up his mind to do something.

"Take time to deliberate, but when the time for action comes, stop thinking and go in."

~**Napoleon Bonaparte**

I'm not saying to be a tyrant and to go overthrow your next-door rival (unless it's a legal move in athletics), but Napoleon's mindset provides a nice segue for the next chapter. We'll see that the world does indeed make room for vertically challenged guys who are willing to speak their mind, act boldly, and follow their passions or talents. Let's call these high achievers men of action. These are guys who have excelled in a number of areas, including sports, business, and entertainment. In many cases, before my research, I wasn't aware such guys were part of our fraternity. It's unfortunate that height bias is so prevalent in society, yet when the vertically challenged reach amazing heights, their height goes without mention.

Chapter-3

Programming and reprogramming

As previously mentioned, the brain comes with software, or heuristics, designed to help us make quick decisions. If we take the initiative, though, we can reprogram our software. Surprisingly, in talking to people, I found out some fraternity members were not concerned about their height or about height bias. The guys who didn't seem to need any reprogramming were in the minority, though. Whether they know it or not, I believe they subconsciously reprogrammed their software over time. And for the record, only one was an actual computer programmer.

Given the average person has about 50,000 thoughts per day, wouldn't it make sense to focus energy on overcoming internal factors instead of trying to change external ones, such as other people's thoughts? Had I known world-renowned icons had climbed to the summit across so many disciplines, I may have been able to reprogram my mind sooner, minimizing internal doubt and blocking out or downplaying doubt coming from external sources.

Tobias van Schneider is a technologist who understands how the mind works. The former creative and product design lead for Spotify creates platforms used by the biggest brands in the world. His article[11] *If You Want It, You Might Get It. The Reticular Activating System Explained* provides a deeper understanding:

"Your RAS takes what you focus on and creates a filter for it. It then sifts through the data and presents only the pieces that are important to you. All of this happens without you noticing, of course. The RAS programs itself to work in your favor without you actively doing anything. Pretty awesome, right?

In the same way, the RAS seeks information that validates your beliefs. It filters the world through the parameters you give it, and your beliefs shape those parameters. If you think you are bad at giving speeches, you probably will be. If you believe you work efficiently, you most likely do. The RAS helps you see what you want to see and in doing so, influences your actions.

Some people suggest that you can train your RAS by taking your subconscious thoughts and marrying them to your conscious thoughts. They call it "setting your intent." This basically means that if you focus hard on your goals, your RAS will reveal the people, information and opportunities that help you achieve them.

If you care about positivity, for example, you will become more aware of and seek positivity. If you really want a pet turtle and set your intent on getting one, you'll tune in to the right information that helps you do that.

When you look at it this way, The Law of Attraction doesn't seem so mystical. Focus on the bad things and you will invite negativity into your life. Focus on the good things and they will come to you, because your brain is seeking them out. It's not magic, it's your Reticular Activating System influencing the world you see around you."

OK, let the knowledge van Schneider is dropping digest for a moment. If you're a self-improvement enthusiast, you may already be on board here. If not, try keeping this in mind as you go about your day. Van Schneider continues with an action plan for training your RAS to get what you want:

1. *Think of the goal or situation you want to influence.*

2. *Think about the experience or result you want to reach in regards to that goal/situation.*

3. *Create a mental movie of how you picture that goal/situation ideally turning out in the future.*

4. *Notice the sounds, conversations, visuals and details of that mental movie. Replay it often in your head.*

We thank you, Tobias. My mindset continues to evolve as a result of life's adventures and character builders. Some of us may want to point the finger (no, not that finger) at society for the pressures of not measuring up to average height or worse, six-foot status (thank you, ladies), or six-foot-plus status (thank you, U.S. political system). Blame game aside, it's likely that half or more of the vertical challenges we face are those we create upstairs, in our minds. That software needs to be reprogrammed, and it's spaghetti code. If enough of us are able to overcome our own preconceived notions around height bias, we can set the stage for others to do so as well, including society at large. A rising tide lifts all boats, so let's rise up.

Fortunately, humans are able to question and reason, allowing us to overcome cognitive biases. Continuing with the computer analogy, this means individuals, including you and I, are able to reprogram the brain's software. This is great for guys on the shorter side: we don't have to succumb to height heuristics and live life as second-class citizens. It also means that society can be rewired. The former is where we can focus our efforts through a trifecta of education, self-awareness, and self-improvement. Even if you're a Master Jedi, it's a heck of a lot easier to manage your way of thinking and behavior than someone else's. Think about it: our vertically challenged crew is 60 million deep in the U.S. alone. If we collectively start upping our games by taking action, society will take note and begin to reprogram those heuristics or false beliefs that being sub-5'10" equates to any "knowns" in life—other than the fact you are a heck of a lot more comfortable flying coach than the poor dude who's 6'3" and kissing his knee caps.

If knowledge is power, then taking time to enhance your awareness of subject matter through reading, audio books and classes, or seminars is a great way to power-up. Become that ace programmer, musical genius or marketing maverick. Another added benefit of continuing education is that people may perceive you as being taller. Consider the following excerpt from Robert Cialdini's book *Influence: The Psychology of Persuasion:*[12]

"Studies investigating the way in which authority status affects perceptions of size have found that prestigious titles lead to height distortions. In one experiment conducted on five classes of Australian college students, a man was introduced as a visitor from Cambridge University in England. However his status at Cambridge was represented differently in each of the classes. To one class he was presented as a student, to a second class, a demonstrator, to another a lecturer, to yet another a senior lecture, to a fifth, a professor. After he left the room, each class was asked to estimate his height. It was found that with each increase in status, the same man grew in perceived height by an average of a half inch. So that as the professor, he was seen as 2 and a half inches taller than the student."

To learn more about the merit of status and intelligence outside of an experiment, with a dash of sophomoric humor, check out the

YouTube video "Can Short Guys Get Hot Girls?" At the 3:15 mark, a couple of girls who are the same height disagree whether a particular professor is taller or shorter than they are. One of them insists he is taller, then proclaims, "He's so sexy and he's so intelligent that it makes up for the height!" This adds merit to the research in Cialdini's book. If you can't be tall, be smart and sexy.

Height may limit opportunities in sports (some more so than others), but there are no height limits for skills like computer programming, foreign languages, mathematics, architecture … the list goes on. Even if you decide midstream that a given topic or area of study isn't as interesting or a passion point like you'd initially thought, the learnings may push you in a new direction that is a better fit. For me, I was pretty solid in math and science during high school, but engineering wasn't quite my jam in college. However, my interests in business and Spanish were an excellent fit for a degree that combined both. It took a semester of being on academic probation due to a 1.57 GPA and having my dad warn me about the prospects of working at McDonald's, but I course-corrected (no pun intended) and eventually got my overall GPA above 3.0. I even landed on the dean's list one semester. Once I found an interesting subject and learned how to study, my college experience became much more enjoyable.

Sometimes you may overcome obstacles by changing the way you think about things, such as the reprogramming associated with false cognitive biases. Other times you may be better served by shifting your focus from one discipline to another. In my case, I realized I wasn't NBA talent, and while college was my best opportunity, I still had to transfer majors before I was on the right path.

From the book *The ONE Thing: The Surprisingly Simple Truth Behind Extraordinary Results* by Gary Keller and Jay Papasan, I was surprised to learn that per multiple research sources, good habits are created in sixty-six days, not thirty days.[13] Let's consider positive habits as the foundation for being able to accomplish bigger things in life. However, if you're looking to power-up or level-up some aspect of your life, passion and skill will likely enter the equation. You may be wondering which is more important. Consider the following excerpt from *The ONE Thing:*

"[Often] the line between passion and skill can be blurry, that's because they're almost always connected."

I may not be the most talented writer or runner; however, developing habits in these areas has allowed me to improve them. Along the way, I uncovered a passion for both. Logging time in either area can be a challenge, but a welcome challenge. Passion provides the fuel needed for me to continue fine-tuning and improving skills. When I began work as an IT analyst, the sea of red ink on my commentaries and reports made my head spin. It was painful, not in the literal sense of course, but I take pride in my work, so the countless errors, questions, and suggested recasts busted my ego. However, I took note and made the necessary adjustments to reduce the editorial process. Ultimately, it was a win-win for me and the rest of the team.

When I began running, I stumbled into yet another learning process. Early on, I endured the occasional side stitch. Anyone who has gotten a side stitch knows they are painful (and typical for rookie runners). For non-runners, a side stich feels like someone jabbing a knife in your ribcage, making it difficult to breathe. It completely messes up your pace. With proper training, I have eliminated these episodes, and I focus on my goals for each race.

There are no height requirements for writing or running. You can be part of a team or do your thing as an individual. Some people love being part of a team, while others find they excel operating on an individual level. As you'll see, team sports tend to favor taller guys, but there are exceptions.

Given height bias is so deeply entrenched in major sports, let's start here and examine some of the factors and considerations. The data tells us that height headwinds vary by sport and by position. In some cases, being undersized can be advantageous. In others, underdogs will only get a shot when their talent and determination converge with the right opportunity, at the right time.

Chapter-4

Sports and Athletics

"If I'm not so large as you, You are not so small as I, And not half so spry."

—Ralph Waldo Emerson

If you are not familiar with Emerson, he was a philosopher and poet. I think his quote holds weight in sports and athletics. As the saying goes, speed kills, and it can be an equalizer when a guy is giving up height to an opponent. Taller guys tend to have an advantage over those of us who are on the shorter side in many sports. This lays the foundation for height bias, starting in grade school. At recess, many times short kids get picked last for kickball. This continues into high school athletics. Anyone who has played basketball, football, baseball, or hockey has likely seen this play out. As a result, many undersized kids get less attention and playing time from coaches. How many guys considered too small or short have been denied athletic opportunities in high school, college, and the pros? Obviously we'll never know.

However, an analysis of current-day rosters in major sports provides an idea of the uphill battle undersized guys face.

Just how many players are under 5'10" in major sports leagues? This chapter provides an overview by professional basketball (NBA), football (NFL), baseball (MLB), hockey (NHL), soccer (MLS) and golf (PGA). Subsequent chapters get into more detail, with sections dedicated to each sport.

Even some of the most gifted athletes in the world face height bias. For example, until his junior year of high school, NFL Hall of Fame running back Barry Sanders was forced to play cornerback because his coach didn't think he was tough enough to play running back.[14] Part of this decision may have been due to Barry's unorthodox style, as he liked to bounce to the outside and get creative, sometimes resulting in loss of yards. However, based on interviews and books, we know Barry's height (5'8") was the main factor. Even today, there are plenty of old-school, hard-nosed, or perhaps narrow-minded coaches out there too stubborn to give undersized guys a chance. Why? Some may argue safety. However in Barry's case and others, coaches are afraid of going against the *conventional wisdom* that smaller guys just can't get the job done as well as bigger guys can. Conventional wisdom would have prevented guys like Barry Sanders, Nate Robinson, or Dustin Pedroia from getting playing time. Fortunately, they encountered coaches who understood that ability goes beyond pure physical attributes. It takes courage for coaches to go against what is generally accepted as *the way* to do things, including what types of players to field certain positions based on size. Rocking the boat and implementing change is risky. A coach, CEO, or other leadership can get fired for making moves that go against the system and fail to deliver results. This is also why most people are content to keep doing the things they've always been doing in life. Change brings uncertainty, and people tend to fear uncertainty. This is just one more reason why the height bias machine remains so prevalent in society.

I started wondering just how and where my (not quite true) claim of 5'9" status originated, then I recalled rosters from my high school baseball, basketball, and football teams. This was the birthplace of my white lie. Perhaps it was just a matter of coaches measuring us with our shoes on. In hindsight, this is just another example of society, specifically high school coaches, fueling the height bias machine. Tall players are preferable for most major sports, as bigger bodies tend to be closer to the rim and to an extent, cover more ground with greater ease. However, when we see short guys making headlines, unfortunately many times height references will be woven into the headlines. Speaking of headlines, there is a trend in the National Hockey League (NHL) towards smaller, faster players, even on defense, which historically skews toward six-foot-plus, 200-pound guys. As a Boston Bruins fan, perhaps I am biased. More to come on this.

Sports that heavily favor taller guys, like basketball, require shorter players to be that much more athletically gifted or talented, typically as scorers. People will see a height difference and stop there. However, factor in wingspan or arm length and this typically doubles the height advantage from a distance to the rim standpoint. Imagine a guy who stands three inches taller than an opponent, then add three inches for the taller guy when their arms are raised above their respective heads, such as when rebounding or shot blocking. This is the main reason height makes such a difference in hoops, as well as in volleyball. Being closer to the rim or net is an advantage. The same case can be made—and typically is—for other sports, such as football, baseball, and hockey.

However, undersized guys can make up for height with quickness, athleticism, and determination. Seeing vertically challenged guys matched up with taller opponents can be incredibly entertaining. Basketball historians will immediately recall Spud Webb, a 5'7" guard for the Atlanta Hawks who won the slam dunk contest in 1986. I can hear Spud now: *Did someone say vertically challenged?*

Ok, so if you're the shorter guy and getting blocked or dominated on the boards, it sucks. I've been there. However when we do score, grab a rebound, or set up a teammate for a score, we earn it just a bit more. Feats such as the spritely Spud Webb winning the slam dunk contest leave an audience, coach, or competitor wondering, "Wait, how'd *that* just happen?!"

If you are looking for inspiration in basketball or running, a couple good books I've read include a biography from former NBA star Nate Robinson (*Heart over Height*) and an autobiography by marathon runner and Boston Marathon Race Director David McGillivray, a die-hard basketball enthusiast (*The Last Pick*). Nate and David are 5'9" and 5'4", respectively.

Anyone who watched Nate Robinson play in the NBA knows he was a scoring machine, backing down from no one. Here are a couple of excerpts from his book:[15]

"When it came to practicing basketball, I was the like the Post Office: I would practice in the rain or sleet or snow. It didn't matter. All I needed was a ball and a hoop and I'd be working on my game somehow . . . I was also blessed with a strong work ethic for things I liked, which allowed me to spend hours practicing sports without a break when other kids would get bored . . . it gave me an edge over other kids my age, even though I was usually smaller."

While this is specific to basketball, it holds true with other sports and can extend to other disciplines, like music, computer programming, and so on. If you have a true passion for something, it will allow you to work through tough conditions, and time will fly.

Writing and fitness are two of my passions. It doesn't matter if it's 8:00 a.m. or 8:00 p.m., I will find myself throwing down a few paragraphs. I write nearly every day, sometimes 500 words, sometimes 2,500 words. It doesn't matter if it gets published or not. I view writing like Nate would view jump shots: It's all about getting repetitions. Lather, rinse, and repeat. Sometimes finding a writing rhythm, even a single sentence, is extremely challenging. Other times I'll go on writing for hours without realizing it. Momentum is a beautiful thing. Once you get into the flow, the zone, or whatever your highest level of performance is, you'll know you've arrived.

I also bring this kind of discipline to my fitness regimen. My day starts with a combination of mind and body activity, typically a combination of meditation and yoga, followed by a walk around the neighborhood. To mix it up, my wake-up regiment will include something intense, say burpees and stair climbers. There is no *will I or won't I?* conversation in my mind; it's a matter of *what* I'm going to write or *what* I'm going to do for exercise. I view these activities as habits. If you find yourself inconsistently applying yourself to a certain area and wish the internal conversation in your mind shifted from a yes/no (which allows for inaction) to a menu or list that creates action, recall earlier in Chapter 3 that it takes sixty-six days to develop a habit. While I haven't run a marathon, I have an idea of the commitment required for endurance events, given the training I did for the Spartan Race at Killington, Vermont. My training began with shorter races, like the Spartan Sprint and Spartan Super, then progressed to three- and four-hour training sessions at Gunstock Mountain in New Hampshire on weekends. These training sessions were almost as fun as the actual event. I met people from all over, including fellow Spartans. When hikers and sightseers learned why I was carrying 50-pound sandbags and buckets up and down the mountain, they offered words of encouragement. Hearing cheers from the chairlift above me while I was grinding it out felt pretty awesome. My goal was sub-five hours, which was within reach, had I not added two miles to the course. In hindsight, getting lost on a massive mountain during an endurance competition is kind of funny, but I'd be lying if I didn't admit to having a moment of panic when it happened. Fortunately, the stars were aligned, and an event volunteer helped me locate the race director. The race director got me back on the course, saving the day. Yes, in addition to being vertically challenged, I am *directionally challenged.*

It's easy to keep going when you're on track, your shot is going in or things are just going your way in general. It's when you hit a rough patch that you find out just how deep your passion goes. Where do you find ongoing interest and endless enthusiasm? Think back to Nate Robinson's dedicated days practicing. When others stop, where do you have the will to keep going? Do you go home when the other kids/colleagues/teammates call it a day, or do you dig in and continue taking reps, making calls, or writing the next line of code? Sometimes, the toughest situation paves the way for truly amazing things in life.

For example, David McGillivray is most well-known for marathons and an epic run from the old Seattle Kingdome to Fenway

Park to raise awareness for The Jimmy Fund, a foundation for research at Boston's Dana-Farber Cancer Institute. However in his book *The Last Pick,* he recalls his love for basketball as a motivating force that ultimately took him down a different path:

"We all have the capacity to make great things happen in our lives, [I'm] not saying there won't be hardships; I've literally been to rock bottom and back again. [When] the high school coach cut me, self-pity could have prevented me from pursuing anything requiring physical ability. Instead, I saw it as a challenge. It was a choice."[16]

An event that forces you to adjust your path, such as getting cut from a team, is not necessarily a failure. The failure label only sticks when you stop trying or completely give up in life. I too was axed from the high school basketball team during my senior year. It was the first and only time I'd ever missed any cut in organized sports of any kind. It was gut-wrenching. I'd been a fairly consistent starter up until my car accident. If coming back from surgery to make the team as a junior was a feel-good story, the sequel was a harsh reality check. Basketball wasn't in the cards. My basketball IQ and hustle were not enough to overcome the fact I was one of the shortest and slowest guys on the court. But after being cut, I had more time to focus on classes, including Spanish, economics, and history. These became some of my favorite classes in high school, as well as college. I attended Clemson University, where I graduated with a degree in Spanish and International Trade. As a kid from New England, I found the whole

Southern culture thing to be an amazing experience. It was like receiving two educations in one. Not making the basketball team was a big deal at the time, but it's now trivial compared to all the life experiences that stemmed from becoming a better student.

Back to height bias in athletics. It cannot be ignored, and for good reason: height does have a direct impact. As McGillivray points out, taller guys tend to get picked first while vertically challenged guys pull up the rear. In the next few chapters, as a reality check, we'll explore how and where the deck is stacked against us shorter guys. The emphasis on size and height starts as early as grade school and typically holds through high school, setting the stage for the select few to compete in college. The average height for NCAA basketball players is 6'4", per ESPN.com. For less than one percent, the opportunity for playing professionally becomes an option. The average height of players in the NBA is 6'7". Meanwhile, average NCAA football players are 6'1", and NFL players are 6'2" on average. Of course, these averages are for two sports that cater to bigger guys. Even if those heights are self-reported, guys under 5'10" likely require an innate ability to compete in the NCAA or NFL, or they possess some combination of speed, strength, or sports IQ that allows them to achieve amazing heights. However, there are sports and instances where being shorter can be beneficial. Let's explore further.

A BBC.com[17] article calls out a favorable factoid for shorter guys in *"Tall vs. Short: Which is Better?"*

"Sometimes a smaller body can be a bonus. It takes less time for a nerve impulse to travel the lengths of their limbs to their brains, meaning that their reaction times should be quicker, and they may be more nimble."

The article goes on to state that bending and twisting a taller body can be more challenging, whereas "smaller people" (aka short guys) can achieve greater rotational acceleration, which gives shorter guys a leg up in gymnastics, snowboarding, skating, skiing, and diving. Those who follow U.S. Olympic winter sports or freestyle snowboarding will recognize the name Shaun White. Nicknamed the Flying Tomato for his red hair, the 5'8" daredevil consistently redefines what going big means. At the 2018 Winter Olympic Games, he made history as the first snowboarder to win three gold medals.

Here's a couple of car metaphors for the fast and furious: consider smaller guys as being equipped with a 4-cylinder turbo engine, whereas taller guys have a V-8 under the hood. We shorter guys tend to be more agile and have better gas mileage, meaning we can go longer distances on less fuel. As I've transitioned from organized sports to running, endurance sports, and hiking, I've noted that my height and weight are an advantage. Taller, heavier guys tend to struggle. To continue with the car talk, consider another quote from the above BBC article:

"Think of your body a bit like a car: in purely mechanical terms, the larger it is, the harder it is to slow down if you need to avoid a collision. What's more, the greater momentum means you face a more painful

impact during collision. And of course, shorter people have less distance to fall. According to one estimate, someone who is 20% taller will build up twice as much kinetic energy during a fall."

This last data point on falling is interesting. Whether you're tall or short, getting knocked down isn't fun. The bigger they are, they harder they fall. Height tends to add weight. Advantage: vertically challenged.

In the NBA, shorter guys that make the squad tend to be gifted scorers, like the Lakers' Isaiah Thomas (5'9") or former NBA star Nate Robinson (5'9"). Although the Phoenix Suns' Tyler Ulis (5'9") doesn't get quite the minutes or brand recognition, he's made his mark by being equally talented in creating scoring opportunities for himself as well as for his teammates. At the time I'm writing this book, Ulis averages 7.4 points and 4.0 assists a game in 23 minutes per game, and the former Kentucky Wildcat is only in his second NBA season. Let's root for this guy.

With only two guys under 5'10" in the NBA, it's going to be an uphill battle. However, basketball has become an international sport. There are plenty of opportunities overseas. Europe has multiple leagues. Italy, anyone?

Call us the underdogs. We can still get the job done through grit, hustle, and determination. As a former hoops guy, you may be wondering if I have a story to share about my basketball days. I sure do. Although not attaining 6'3" status stunted my scoring prowess, and a car accident further dented my hoops hopes, my intramural games in college were competitive and provided the occasional vertically challenged highlight. For the record, universities tend to have some pretty solid intramural players. I rarely hit double-digit scoring, but I enjoyed playing D, and in one memorable game, I chased down a guy who'd stolen the ball at midcourt and thought he could coast in for a layup. Timing was good, and I proceeded to pound his shot off the backboard, LeBron James style. (OK, with perhaps slightly less airtime.) This taller guy, probably six-foot or so, was absolutely irate and got a technical foul. My memory fades here, but it could have been due to the fact Iain, our 6'7" Bermudian center yelled, "That's the illest block I've ever seen!" loud enough for the entire gym to hear. My Pi Kapp fraternity brother was invited to try out for Clemson's basketball team, so bear with me here as I puff up a bit. Nearly a decade later at a Clemson football game, I met up with Iain, and he replayed the scene as we reminisced. True story. Now, was it as jaw-dropping as Spud Webb doing a 360-degree dunk in the Slam Dunk Championship? Hardly. However, I promised a few personal anecdotes would be added to the mix of high flyers. If Spud were coaching us and keeping stats at the time, he would be pleased.

Back to addressing the vertical challenge. Chapters 5 through 10 review major professional sports leagues in the United States: basketball, football, baseball, hockey, and golf. Included are figures on

46

the total number of players under 5'10" as well as highlights of top performers. As you'll see from the data, height bias is more prevalent in some professional sports leagues than in others.

Chapter-5

National Basketball Association (NBA)

If you recall, there are two NBA players 5'9" or under. Based on active rosters and 390 total players, this equates to 0.5% of the league being vertically challenged.

The number of guys by position who are 5'9" or under:

- Forwards: 0

- Centers: 0

- Guards: 2

Just because there are only a couple of shorter guys currently in the league doesn't mean there haven't been others who've achieved greatness in the past. Let's start with a quote from a guy who could light up the scoreboard and get vertical:

"God blessed me with a lot of heart and no height, and I'll take that any day."

- Nate Robinson, New York *Knicks* (5'9" with shoes)

The incidence rate of guys under 5'10" in the NBA (half of one percent) is what it is: a statistic. History tells us that unless you have ridiculous talent, a big heart, and serious athleticism, the NBA tends to turn a cold shoulder on the vertically challenged. Calvin Murphy is currently the shortest NBA player in the Naismith Memorial Basketball Hall of Fame. At 5'9", Murphy played in the '70s and early 80s for the San Diego/Houston Rockets. Eventually, I think we'll see the Cleveland Cavaliers' Isaiah Thomas (also 5'9") join him, but for now, Murphy is our only guy in the hall. He received 235 college scholarships and chose to attend Niagara University. He averaged 33 points a game during his career. While Niagara isn't a household hoops name by today's standards, they did play Syracuse and other big schools. Calvin dropped over 60 on the 'Cuse one year and earned All-American honors three times.

Calvin Murphy, Guard, 5'9", 165 lbs

"[He was] like a bantamweight who dared to make his living in the heavyweight division."

~ Rockets teammate Major Jones

NBA stats during Murphy's 13-year career:

- Games: 1,002

- Points per game: 17.9

- Assists per game: 4.4

- Steals per game: 1.5

- Free throw %: 89.2* (78 consecutive free throws made ranks third all-time)

And the icing on the cake: Murphy was inducted into the Naismith Memorial Basketball Hall of Fame in 1993.

Spud Webb, Guard, 5'7", 132 lbs

As we previously mentioned, height plus wingspan (i.e. reach) make hoops a sport for the vertically gifted. However, that didn't stop Anthony Gerome "Spud" Webb. Hall of Famer Murphy would be a pseudo-giant compared to Webb, who at 5'7" was consistently told he was too short to play basketball. He received a chance to play on his junior high team only after two players forgot to complete their physical exam requirements in time for the first game. Webb scored 20 points in that game. He could dunk the ball when he was only 5'3". Webb went to Midland Community College for two years before enrolling at North Carolina State, where he'd average over 10 points and 5 assists per game. Not too shabby. It's also worth noting that in his first year, he blocked 10 shots, or roughly one for every three games. Most dudes were probably more focused on his 5'6" frame than his 42" vertical jump. For comparison, Michael "Air" Jordan's vertical jump was 40".

NBA stats during Webb's 13-year career:

- Games: 814

- Points per game: 9.9

- Assists per game: 5.3

- Steals per game: 1.1

For you youngsters, search YouTube for the 1986 Slam Dunk contest. In the finals, Webb goes up against Hawks teammate Dominique Wilkins, who is 6'8" and nicknamed the "Human Highlight Film" due to his superhuman abilities. Webb bests Wilkins—it was absolutely amazing. Most of the players had thought Webb could dunk, but that it wouldn't be show-stopping material. They were wrong.

Nate Robinson, Guard, 5'9", 180 lbs

Being the class act he is, Spud decided he would pass the torch by providing guidance to the 5'9" Nate Robinson, who went on to win the contest in 2006, 2008, and 2009. Robinson is playing in Europe these days but posted stats similar to Webb during Webb's glory days, with solid performances playing for the Knicks, Celtics, and Warriors. As a Knick, Robinson scored a career-high 45 points in one game, plus torched the net with 23 points in one quarter while playing with the Bulls (Michael Jordan holds the franchise record with 24). Nate tells his story in his book *Heart over Height,* a good read for basketball enthusiasts facing heightism, or athletes playing other sports who are looking for a boost.

NBA stats during Robinson's 14-year career:

- Games: 618

- Points per game: 11.0

- Assists per game: 3.0

- Steals per game: 0.9

Tyrone Curtis "Muggsy" Bogues, Guard, 5'3", 137 lbs

The most vertically challenged NBA player. *Ever.*

Bogues attended Wake Forest University, where he provided a combination of offense and defense, averaging 14.8 points, 9.5 assists and 2.4 steals per game. This set the stage for being drafted twelfth by the Washington Bullets in 1987-88. The following year he went to the Charlotte Hornets as part of the expansion draft. He was known as one of the fastest players on the court. Bogues's speed, basketball

IQ, and athleticism made him fun to watch when I was growing up. He reportedly had a 44" vertical; however, small hands didn't allow him to grip the ball well enough to dunk.

NBA stats during Bogues's 15-year career:

- Games: 889

- Points per game: 7.7

- Assists per game: 7.6

- Steals per game: 1.6

Not only was Bogues a dual threat on the court, he took his game to new heights off the court. After the NBA, Bogues made his rounds in the entertainment circuit, appearing on *Curb Your Enthusiasm, Space Jam,* and even *Saturday Night Live.* Yes, Bogues was a talented hoops player who may have been presented a few cool opportunities, but if he wasn't open-minded or didn't have an interest, those chances would have passed him by. Like Muggsy, maybe you've got a skill set that you can parlay, maybe using a capability or a persona to gain inroads into another? I try to be on the lookout for opportunities whenever I'm speaking to people. And I don't always look for the power brokers. Those who need support or guidance may someday be the ones who help you level-up in life. Besides, helping others is part of the Golden Rule ... plus karma is a mighty force.

OK, let's review. There are just two players 5'9" or under in the NBA as of the writing of this book—or fewer than 1 percent of all NBA players. Calvin Murphy is the only guy in the Hall of Fame 5'9" or under. The ten-foot goal gives the advantage to taller players, but there are opportunities for guys who can light it up scoring and dishing assists. Perhaps there is another Mighty Mouse in the making reading this? For those who don't know, that's a reference to former NBA Guard Damon Stoudamire, who was consistently listed at 5'10" … meaning he potentially could have been another inductee into our hall of fame.

Chapter-6

National Football League (NFL)

During the 2008 NFL playoffs, Darren Sproles helped the San Diego Chargers make a late-season run to make the playoffs. An ESPN.com article by Greg Garber gave a shout out to the 5'6" Sproles and noted that 1.6 percent of NFL players were 5'8" or shorter (27 of 1,700 players). As the 2017 playoffs approached, I figured it was time to see if things had changed. Doing an apples-to-apples comparison, only counting players up to 5'8", the findings were somewhat positive. There were 33 players up to 5'8" on rosters, or 1.9 percent. Over a 10-year span, that's a 22 percent increase—but a relatively small sample size. However, if we include the 57 players at 5'9" on 2017 rosters, the total jumps to 90 players, or 5.3 percent. Compared to the NBA, the NFL door is slightly more ajar for undersized guys.

The number of players by position:

- Running back: 18

- Wide receiver: 11

- Kicker: 2

- Cornerback: 1

- Safety: 1

What does this tell us? Clearly the opportunities tend to be on the offensive side of the ball. A dash of speed plus the shiftiness of shorter guys allows us to be an asset. However, the door is open on defense, too. Just ask a few of the guys who had to face Darrell Green. As offense tends to get the limelight, let's start with impact guys on defense. Who better than Green?

Darrell Green, Cornerback, 5'9", 184 lbs

Green played twenty years in the NFL and is considered one of the best cover cornerbacks ever (think "shut down" guy, or the one tasked with covering the opponent's best wide receiver). Growing up in Texas, Green was a track star who nicknamed himself the "Itty Bitty Guy". Others called him the "Ageless Wonder" given that he played in the league until he was forty-two years old, always with the Washington Redskins. Two decades of playing football is impressive. With the same team? Added wow factor.

Green's accomplishments include:

- Career interceptions: 54

- NFL record with consecutive seasons, one or more interceptions: 19 years

- Super Bowl Champion (1987, 1991)

- Pro Bowl (1984, 1986, 1991, 1996, 1997)

- NFL Walter Payton Man of the Year (1996)

- Pro Football Hall of Fame inductee (2008)

- NFL's Fastest Man competition winner (1986, 1988, 1989 and 1991)

He took considerable pride in being the fastest man the league and wasn't afraid to mix in a little humor with the badge:

"I am the fastest man in the NFL. I am faster than all the players. I am faster than all the coaches. I am faster than all the general managers, trainers and the PR men. I am the fastest man in the NFL."

~ Darrell Green

The Ageless Wonder continued to defy. On his fiftieth birthday in 2010, he reportedly clocked a 40-yard run in 4.43 seconds. Mr. Green, you are an inspiration for little guys and older guys alike.

Let's move to the offensive side of the ball, shall we?

Barry Sanders, Running Back, 5'8" (per NFL combine, 5'7 and 5/8")

"Too often we are scared. Scared of what we might not be able to do. Scared of what people might think if we tried. We let our fears stand in the way of our hopes."

~ Barry Sanders

Considered by many (including myself) to be one of the best running backs (RBs) ever, Barry Sanders played ten years in the NFL. On his way to stardom, Sanders had to continually disprove to people that his performance on the field would be limited by his height. Up until his senior year in high school, he was forced to cornerback because his coach didn't think he was tough enough for running back (not that there's anything wrong with cornerback). His coach didn't appreciate Sanders's ability to, shall we say, improvise at the line of scrimmage. Fortunately a new head coach allowed Sanders to excel in his senior year, one that allowed him to play running back and work his magic, evading would-be tacklers two, three, and four at a time.

Sanders's short stature, combined with his speed and power and made-for-video-game moves made him unique and created challenges for defenders. As of December 2017, Sanders is one of only seven running backs to rush for 2,000 or more yards in a season. For me, one of the coolest things about Sanders was the fact he never spiked the football. He'd break 10 tackles and run 80 yards for a touchdown, then casually hand the football to the referee. Just doing his job. Not surprising that this is the same person who preferred to let teammates get playing time instead of chasing individual records. Speaking of records, here are some accomplishments and numbers to review:

- NFL combine performance: 4.41 40-yard dash and 41.5" vertical jump
- NFL Hall of Fame inductee (2005)
- 3rd all-time leading rusher (15,269 yards)
- 10 consecutive seasons 1,000+ yards
- 14 consecutive 100+ yard games
- 1989 Rookie of the Year
- 1990 NFC Rushing Title
- 1991 NFL Rushing Title
- 1997 NFL MVP

Source: BarrySanders.com

One story I like goes back to Sanders's high school days in Kansas. During his final year, he had an opportunity to capture the state rushing title. When his coach asked if he wanted to pad the proverbial stats during the season finale, the star running back opted to let the younger guys get some playing time. Talk about a class act.

I think he's a great example of someone who did everything for the team and was all about winning.

If you're looking for a player under 5'10" in more recent times, Maurice Jones-Drew demonstrated a similar mindset in overcoming height bias:

Maurice Jones-Drew, Running Back, 5'7", 208 lbs

"I can't grow any taller, all I can do, and I believe it, is go out there and play like I'm 6'3" ... and however many pounds they want me to weigh."

- ~ Maurice Jones Drew (MJD)
- Pro Bowl (2009, 2010, 2011)
- NFL Rushing Leader (2011)
- 1,000+ yards rushing (2009, 2010, 2011
- 8,167 career rushing yards, 2,944 receiving yards, 79 total touchdowns
- NFL combine: 4.49 seconds 40-yard dash, 36" vertical

Source: MauriceDrew.com

Going back to the analysis of players by position, it would make sense for us sticks of dynamite to pursue running back or cornerback positions. Of course, there are exceptions and outliers—some guys with a cannon for an arm who love to throw the pigskin should make a go at QB. Speaking of QBs, let's take a look at the shortest guy to line up under center in the NFL.

Doug Flutie, Quarterback, 5'9", 180 lbs (listed as 5'10" during playing days but admitted during an interview to being 5'9" and change)

"It's my whole life of being the little guy and having a little chip on my shoulder, from year to year trying to prove myself, and at the end of the day to be inducted into the College Football Hall of Fame is a very special honor for me."

~Doug Flutie

In 1984, Boston College QB Doug Flutie made headlines when he threw a Hail Mary to beat the number-one-ranked team in the nation. That year, he won the Heisman Trophy and the Davey O'Brien National Quarterback Award. He went on to play QB in the NFL for the Buffalo Bills, San Diego Chargers, Chicago Bears, and New England Patriots.

Flutie's NFL accolades include:

- NFL Pro Bowl (1998)

- NFL Comeback Player of the Year (1998)

- Passing yards: 14,715

- Rushing yards: 1,634

- Passing touchdowns: 86

- Rushing touchdowns: 10

However, he did the most statistical damage in our sister league to the north, the Canadian Football League (CFL), winning the Grey Cup (Canada's equivalent to the Super Bowl) in 1992, 1996, and 1997. He also won the Most Valuable Player (MVP) Award six times (1991-1994, 1996, and 1997).

Now, as a New England native and someone who frequents the Boston area, I had the pleasure of seeing Flutie at the tail end of a charity function downtown. As I walked past, I noted that we were nearly the same height. Further research plus his own admission during a radio talk show indicate he was actually 5'9". It's been over a decade since Flutie laced up in the NFL and he is *still* the shortest QB ever. Additional bragging rights include converting a drop kick for an extra point against the Miami Dolphins in 2006. The esoteric play requires that the ball bounce on the ground before being booted through the uprights. Flutie is the only player to accomplish the feat since 1941. Mr. Flutie, in addition to your current accolades, we'll induct you into *our* Hall of Fame.

Let's review. There are 90 players 5'9" or under in the NFL as of the writing of this book. With practice squads included, that figure may be double. Just because you're under 5'10" doesn't mean you are necessarily relegated to a specific position, but I'd go out on a limb and say that high-skill positions such as cornerback or wide receiver would be an easier path than being a lineman. Perhaps the NFL's next five-foot-something QB is reading this?

Chapter-7

Major League Baseball (MLB)

T he most vertically challenged player to be inducted into the National Baseball Hall of Fame in Cooperstown is Willie Keeler. At 5'4" and 140 lbs, Keeler "had one *of the biggest bats in the game, both figuratively and literally, weighing up to 46 ounces.*"[18] Nicknamed "Wee Willie," there was nothing small about Keeler's performance. He hit over .300 in 13 seasons, batting .424 in 1897, a record for left-handed hitters.

As of the end of the 2017 season, 40 players are listed on MLB.com at 5'9" or under, or 4.6 percent. Here's a breakdown by position:

- Infielders: (1B, 2B, 3B or SS): 16

- Outfielders (LF, RF, CF): 15

- Pitchers (starters or relievers): 6

- Catchers: 3

Teams with the most players 5'9" or under (3 teams with 4 players):

- Boston Red Sox: Mookie Betts, Tzu-Wei Lin, Dustin Pedroia, Christian Vazquez

- Toronto Blue Jays: Gift Ngoepe, Marcus Stroman, Raffy Lopez, Devon Travis

- Texas Rangers: Willie Calhoun, Matt Bush, Juan Cedeno, Delino DeShields

Teams without any players 5'9" or under (6 teams):

- Minnesota Twins

- Chicago Cubs

- Cincinnati Reds

- Milwaukee Brewers

- Arizona Diamondbacks

- San Francisco Giants

While sifting through the data, I noted that 22 position players (non-pitchers) either batted left-handed or were switch hitters. This equates to 55 percent. In comparison, the overall percentage of MLB players who are left-handed is about 25 percent. While this isn't quite an apples-to-apples comparison, it does highlight that guys under average height have a higher tendency to be a switch hitter (especially infielders) or a natural southpaw (for outfielders).

How do things compare if we look back a decade to 2007? There were 43 players 5'9" or shorter. Given the relatively small sample size, it's tough to say whether height bias is preventing guys from getting the call. With that said, it's worth noting that ten years ago, there were two players 5'6" (David Eckstein and Donnie Sadler) and two players 5'8" (Chone Figgins and Maicer Izturis). Eckstein, Sadler, and Figgins all played for the Los Angeles Angels. Meanwhile, the Philadelphia Phillies had the most players (four), who were 5'9" or under: Tom Gordon, Jimmy Rollins, Shane Victorino, and Fabio Castro. When one underdog proves his capabilities to an organization, I think the coaches on that team give stronger consideration to guys of similar stature. This creates the clusters of shorter players we see today. So if you're an undersized guy coming up through the ranks and being pursued by scouts, I think it's worthwhile to focus on teams that already acknowledge that greatness can come in a variety of sizes.

Dustin Pedroia, Boston Red Sox, Second Base, 5'9", 175 lbs

"People always ask me if I wish I were bigger. I tell them no. I always wanted to be a miniature badass."

~Dustin Pedroia

Pedroia's accolades include:

- Rookie of the Year, AL (2007)

- American League MVP (2008)

- Gold Glove (2008, 2011, 2013, 2014)

- Silver Slugger (2008)

- World Series Champion (2007, 2013)

In addition to being a statistical freak show and knocking out line drive hits that resemble a laser show, Pedroia embodies what baseball is all about. But don't take it from me: consider that in 2013, he won the Heart & Hustle Award, given each year by the Major League Baseball Players Alumni Association (MLBPAA) to an active player who not only excels on the field, but also "best embodies the values, spirits and traditions of baseball."[19]

Even if you're not a Red Sox fan like me, "Pedey," as he's affectionately known in Red Sox Nation, has gained respect for the tenacity he brings to every game. Let's check out another guy who has overcome baseball's height bias:

José Altuve, Houston Astros, Second Base, 5'6", 165 lbs

If you watched postseason baseball in 2017, then you know Altuve was a force to be reckoned with. En route to winning the regular season American League MVP (beating out Aaron Judge, who's a foot taller, by the way) and helping the Houston Astros win the 2017 World Series, he batted .310 and hit seven home runs—three in one game against the Red Sox:

- AL batting title (2014, 2016, and 2017)

- AL All-Star (2012, 2014, 2015, 2016, 2017)

- AL stolen bases leader (2014, 2015)

- Golden Glove (2015)

- Sports Illustrated Sportsperson of the Year (2017)

- Associated Press Athlete of the Year (2017)

In addition, he's hit 24 home runs the last two years. Altuve isn't just a small, speedy guy who slaps singles—he also hits for power.

This is all pretty amazing considering as a sixteen-year-old, Altuve was not called back after an initial tryout with the Astros while living in Venezuela. He attended a tryout with about fifty other guys and, showing his courage and belief in his abilities, showed up the following day even though he didn't get an invite. His determination allowed him to overcome the perception scouts and others had that a 5'6" guy wouldn't be able to compete.

In *Bleacher Report*,[20] the AL MVP shares the mindset it took for him to make it to the big leagues:

"I never doubted myself because I already had too many other people doubting," Altuve says. "I wanted to prove those people wrong. And not because one day I could tell them they were wrong. I wanted to prove them wrong for the guys behind me who are short, too. Guys who are not really strong, not really tall, guys who are 14 to 16 right now who are very small and want to get an opportunity. And I know maybe after that happened to me scouts now will think twice before telling someone, *You're not going to make it.* They're going to think, *This guy is the same size as José, and if Jose made it, maybe one of these guys can make it, too.*"

This goes to show that even if the deck is stacked against smaller guys in baseball, opportunity will knock for those with the talent and willingness to persevere.

"If I open at least one door, two doors, three doors for guys behind me, I'm going to feel like everything that I did, it was because of this, and that will feel good."

~ José Altuve

Guys like Pedroia and Altuve have opened doors for sure. However, I think it's worth noting there were guys before these two that helped open people's minds, even just a crack. After discovering his combination of speed and power, the Minnesota Twins drafted one of the all-time greats, Kirby Puckett.

Kirby Puckett, Minnesota Twins, Center Field, 5'8", 178 lbs

"I was told I would never make it because I'm too short. Well, I'm still too short. It doesn't matter what your height is, it's what's in your heart."

-Kirby Puckett

Puckett's accolades include:

- Career batting average: .318 (53rd all-time)

- Hits: 2,304

- Home runs: 207

- RBIs: 1,085

- AL Batting Champion (.339 average in 1989)

- AL RBI leader (112 in 1994)

- AL All-Star (10 times, 1986–1995)

- Gold Glove (1986–1989, 1991, 1992)

- Baseball Hall of Fame (2001)

Puckett had excellent timing and just enough speed, which allowed him to rob more than his fair share of extra base hits as well as home runs. Puckett also earned the Roberto Clemente Award. This is given to a player who best exemplifies the game of baseball, sportsmanship, community involvement, and the individual's contribution to his team. Unfortunately, Puckett's Hall of Fame career was cut short due to glaucoma in 1996, and he died at the early age of forty-five due from a stroke.

Jim Rantz, the Minnesota Twins' farm system director credited with scouting Puckett one summer, had this to say about Puckett:

"[What] impressed me the most was the way he carried himself on and off the field. It was like 90 degrees or more and everyone else was dragging around. He was the first one on the field and the first one off. You could see he enjoyed playing, he was having fun . . . [The] one knock on him was his size; everyone thought he was too small. Again, as Kirby went along, he got a little bigger (at the time he was 165 pounds), but no one knew how big his heart was."[21]

Puckett is another example of a guy who held his own on the field, and I wasn't surprised to hear he was a class act away from the field. Kirby took a year away from school and baseball to help support his family, installing carpets in a factory. A super talented guy who put his family first. If you haven't seen his highlights, you're missing out and should check him out on YouTube. Kirby had wheels, power, and a true passion for the game that allowed him to achieve greatness. A man of action on multiple levels.

So let's review. There are forty players 5'9" or under in MLB, as of the writing of this book. I think it's a safe bet that there are couple hundred or so in the minor leagues (e.g. rookie, A, AA, and AAA). Vertically challenged guys can hit for average and power, make all-star teams, and help teams win World Series. In 2017, MLB's shortest player, José Altuve (5'6") was voted the best player in the American League. Now that we've established the fact that guys who are on the shorter side can play at the highest of levels, let's transition from the diamond to the gridiron.

Chapter-8
National Hockey League (NHL)

Similar to the percentages in pro baseball, about 50 percent of NHL players under 5'10" shoot left-handed. However, what's different about hockey—and there is plenty of debate on the subject—is that overall, 70 percent of the league shoots left-handed. This is a benefit of playing with the dominant hand at the top of the stick. For comparison, right-handed hitters in baseball would have to swap hand positions on a hockey stick, making them lefties. Make sense? Try it out sometime. This means most of the guys under 5'9" are likely natural lefties.

Of the roughly 700 players on NHL.com, there are 28 players or 3.9 percent of the league who are 5'9" or shorter.

The number of NHL guys by position who are 5'9" or under:

- Forwards: 16

- Centers: 7

- Defensemen: 5

- Goalies: 0

Being from New Hampshire, I know the Boston Bruins have a dynamic duo of small but mighty studs on their roster. Defensemen Torey Krug and forward Brad Marchand are five-niners (both are 5'9"). For those familiar with Marchand, he is a polarizing player, to say the least. He's earned the nickname "Little Ball of Hate." He's also a scoring machine, though his edgy play earns him a stream of penalty box minutes and even suspensions. Opposing fans will say his move was an intentional stick to the groin, Bruins fans see an unfortunate collision. Other times, Brad has been known to display signs of affection towards opponents that isn't well-received.

What's cool about Marchand and Krug is they are essentially polar opposites. Marchand was highly ranked and the No. 71 overall pick in the 2006 NHL draft. Meanwhile, Krug, although respected, was an undrafted free agent who signed with Boston in 2012. Different backgrounds and trajectories, but both led players to reach amazing heights.

Brad Marchand, Boston Bruins, Forward, 5'9", 181 lbs

NHL career stats and accolades for Marchand:

- Games: 567

- Goals: 210

- Assists: 205

- Stanley Cup (2010)

- Gold Medal World Cup of Hockey (2016)

Torey Krug, Boston Bruins, Defenseman, 5'9", 186 lbs

NHL career stats and accolades for Krug:

- Games: 359

- Goals: 44

- Assists: 154

Looking beyond his on-the-ice prowess: Marchand has also been recognized for charitable contributions, receiving the John P. Bucyk Award. He's also been named one of the "Most Stylish Bostonians" by The Boston Globe.[22] Style counts, especially for vertically challenged guys.

Of course, there are other vertically challenged guys who play hockey in the NHL. Three that must be called out for their ability to achieve amazing heights (and to show I'm not a total homer) are Jared Spurgeon, Johnny Gaudreau, and Cam Atkinson.

If we look at height and weight, Jared Spurgeon of the Minnesota Wild is the smallest defenseman in the league. In 2017, he had arguably one of the team's prettiest goals of the season, catching a shot that deflected off the goal then tossing it waist-high and batting it into the net. Ridiculous hand-eye coordination.

Jared Spurgeon, Minnesota Wild, Defenseman, 5'9", 168 lbs

NHL career stats for Spurgeon:

- Games: 485
- Goals: 52
- Assists: 139

Johnny Gaudreau is another elite, per ESPN hockey analyst Chris Peters:

"Since he came into the league, Calgary Flames winger Johnny Gaudreau has been my favorite player to watch by a pretty large margin. I think he's the best and most creative puck handler in the game today, and combines that with spectacular vision and hockey sense. That mix, in addition to his quickness, has allowed the talented winger to overcome the fact that he stands at a generously listed 5-foot-9 and 157 pounds. It also makes him incredibly entertaining when the puck is on his stick. Even when a play seems broken, "Johnny Hockey" can make something out of it."[23]

My dad is not an ESPN analyst, but he is one of the biggest all-around hockey fans I know. We're talking about the kind of person that goes to pro and college games, even if the teams he roots for aren't playing. He struck up a conversation with Johnny Hockey's old *figure skating* coach during a collegiate game at the Herb Brooks Arena in Lake Placid, New York. Yes, it's safe to say that one of the NHL's biggest studs developed some of his craftiest moves by learning figure skating techniques. By combining his size and talent with perhaps slightly less conventional moves, the Calgary Flames winger became one of the fastest and *prettiest* offensive players on the ice.

Upon further review, Gaudreau has moxie and business sense. For example, he patented the term *Johnny Hockey*. The United States Trademark and Patent office granted him rights as of 2016. A smaller guy who's climbed the ranks by making his size a strength, not a weakness, Gaudreau is recognized as one of the most exciting players in the league. Score another for the underdogs.

Johnny Gaudreau, Calgary Flames, Forward, 5'9", 157 lbs

NHL career stats for Johnny Hockey:

- Games: 277

- Goals: 88

- Assists: 170

Last but not least, consider the Columbus Blue Jackets' right winger Cam Atkinson as another guy who's making it known that bigger isn't always better.

Cam Atkinson, Columbus Blue Jackets, Forward, 5'8", 179 lbs

NHL career stats for Atkinson:

- Games: 414

- Goals: 127

- Assists: 113

An interview with NHL.com provides a glimpse into the mindset that's allowed Atkinson to excel:

"Everyone at every single age, every single level, told me I wouldn't make it to the next level. So I think that's kind of fueled my fire, for sure. Obviously being a smaller guy, you have to have a little arrogance to your game. That's what's made me the person, the player, I am today."[24]

This is the type of tenacity and mindset that allows guys to overcome height bias, or the vertical challenge, if you prefer. Identify your passion(s) and then find the fuel to keep them going. Doubters or haters may even be part of what you add to the tank.

Chapter-9

Major League Soccer (MLS)

One of the major requisites of soccer, unless you're playing goalie, is that you need to get up and down the field—a lot. Remember the car engine analogy I made earlier? Well, smaller guys, or the 4-cylinder turbo engines, tend to be a good fit for the endurance requirements of soccer. It makes sense that of the professional team-based sports, Major League Soccer (MLS) is the most welcoming for the vertically challenged. Later, we'll look at the PGA for you fans of the individual sports.

In MLS as of 2017, 150 players are listed at 5'9" or under, or 29.7 percent. Here's a breakdown by position, based on data from MLS.com:

- Forwards: 18

- Midfielders: 85

- Midfielders/Forwards: 8

- Defensemen/Midfielders: 4

- Defensemen: 34

- Goalies: 1

Based on the data, learning to play midfield is the most frequent path, while tending goal could be a significant challenge. The midfielder position will typically log more miles than any other position, while center midfielder is particularly critical as they set the tempo and quarterback plays for offense and defense. Let's check out some of the guys who are fleet of feet and making headlines in MLS.

Hailing from Italy and nicknamed *Atomic Ant* (after the cartoon character), Sebastian Giovinco has the distinction of being one of the smallest and best players in MLS. His team, Toronto FC, invested in ways that allow Sebastian to maximize his speed, quickness, and shot-making ability. As a result, he's put up incredible seasons in his nascent MLS career. In 2015, his first year in the league, he broke the league's scoring record en route to winning the Golden Boot, an award for the most goals and assists.

Sebastian Giovinco, Toronto FC, Midfielder, 5'4", 135 lbs

MLS career stats and accolades for Giovinco:

- Games: 85

- Goals: 55

- Assists: 37

- Shots: 486

- Shots on goal (SOG): 184

- MLS Golden Boot (2015)

- MLS Newcomer of the Year (2015)

- MLS MVP (2015)

While height bias can favor taller guys in sports and business—and MLS is certainly a business—Giovinco is overcoming that bias on *both* fronts. He makes $7.1 million a year,[25] the second-highest salary in the league. Score another for the vertically challenged guy.

Bradley Wright-Phillips, New York Red Bulls, Forward, 5'8", 155 lbs

The product of England could be considered undersized; however, in MLS, Wright-Phillips is a beast. Prior to rising to stardom, Bradley was simply viewed as the younger brother of Shaun (5'5"), who had made a name for himself in England's Premier League. We won't get into talent wars, but let's just say the Premier League has a leg up on American MLS.

MLS career stats and accolades for Wright Phillips:

- Games: 139

- Goals: 86

- Assists: 16

- Shots: 420

- Shots on goal: 206

- MLS Golden Boot (2014 and 2016, the only 2-time winner)

Before we exit the land of futbol, let's check out a guy who redefines quick and may pass you by if you blink. He's only been in MLS for a year, previously playing in Liga MX, Mexico's professional soccer league, helping his team win multiple titles.

Maximiliano "Maxi" Moralez, New York City FC, Midfielder, 5'2", 115 lbs

Career stats for Moralez:

- Games: 29

- Goals: 5

- Assists: 9

- Shots: 44

- Shots on goal: 17

Maxi Moralez is a playmaking dynamo, or as some say in Spanish, a *frascuito* (little flask). If you're wondering, Moralez isn't just a utility guy that gets minimal playing time. He's making $2 million per year, making him the thirteenth highest-paid player in MLS. Suffice it to say, Maxi's focus on ball control and killer moves allow him to climb the ranks at any level.

OK, let's review. There are 150 players 5'9" or under in MLS. With three out of every ten players being part of our fraternity, MLS is the major U.S. sports league that's the least discriminating when it comes to height (we'll review golf, an individual sport, next). If you are a goaltender, the deck is stacked against you, while midfielder tends to be the position where shorter guys get the most opportunity. This makes sense given the vast space covered by midfielders, making your endurance, speed, and quickness real assets. Midfielders play a crucial role as they control the pace and tempo of the game. Meanwhile, being taller and taking up more space is advantageous for goalies.

Chapter-10

Professional Golf Association (PGA)

The vertical challenge is more deeply ingrained in some professional sports than in others. Based on the percentage of players under the 5'10" benchmark, we've identified that the NBA is the least likely place for guys of our fraternity to break the ranks, while MLS has the highest percentage of five-footers. Pro golf is unique; it's an individual sport, and from my seat, golf is egalitarian—or the sport least discriminatory based on physical attributes. However, while some may not view golf as a true sport, I'd argue that strength and athleticism are part of the program. Try and walk 18 holes sometime.

Of the 92 active players listed on PGA.com, 18 guys are under 5'10", which is 19.5 percent of the total roster. A quick note: there are 125 players eligible, however as of January 2018 PGA.com only lists profiles for 92 players. The law of physics does give taller guys the benefit when it comes to driving the ball; however, there is also the old golf adage that the woods are full of long hitters.

Before we check out current guys on tour, let's review some of the legends. Gene Sarazen played in the 1920s and 1930s. He passed away in 1999, but his story is impressive even today. At 5'5", his height did not prevent him from dominating the sport. He was born Eugenio Saraceni, but changed his name because Gene Sarazen sounded more like a golfer's name. How's that for dedication? During the final round of the Masters Tournament in 1933, Sarazen sunk a 235-yard par-5 (a double eagle) that allowed him to leapfrog the leader, who had been up by three shots. The tournament officials had already made the check out to Craig Wood, who was leading Sarazen by three strokes. This improbable shot allowed Sarazen to win and became known as "the shot hear around the world."[26]

Gene Sarazen 5'5", 161 lbs

Career PGA accolades for Sarazen include:

- PGA Tour Wins: 39 (11th all-time)

- Masters Tournament (1935)

- U.S. Open (1922, 1932)

- The Open Championship (1932)

- PGA Championship (1922, 1923, 1933)

- World Golf Hall of Fame (1974)

- Credited for developing the sand wedge

"The more I practice, the luckier I get."

~ Gene Sarazen

Luck is where preparation and opportunity meet. Sarazen's passion for the game was so strong that he changed his name. Can you imagine the countless hours of practice he put in to master his craft?

Let's check out another legend.

At the age of twenty-nine, Gary Player won the 1965 U.S. Open and became the only non-American to win all four majors, known as the Career Grand Slam.[27] For non-golfers, the Grand Slam refers to the Masters Tournament, the U.S. Open, The Open Championship and PGA Championship. Along with Arnold Palmer and Jack Nicklaus, Player is often referred to as one of the "Big Three" golfers of his era, from the late 1950s through the late 1970s. He was branded a "traitor" by South African National Party (NP) government supporters for inviting and bringing both black tennis pro Arthur Ashe and golfer Lee Elder to play in South Africa. In addition to being one of the Big Three, Player's accomplishments earned him three nicknames: the Black Knight, Mr. Fitness, and the International Ambassador of Golf.

Gary Player 5'6", 150 lbs

Career PGA accolades for Player include:

- Masters Tournament (1961, 1974, 1978)

- U.S. Open (1965)

- The Open Championship (1959, 1968, 1974)

- PGA Championship (1962, 1972)

- World Golf Hall of Fame (1974)

- PGA Tour Lifetime Achievement Award (2012)

He is one of five players (with Ben Hogan, Gary Player, Jack Nicklaus, and Tiger Woods) to win each of the four majors at least once, now known as the Career Grand Slam.

How about a two-for-one? Brian Harman is currently the least vertically gifted guy on the PGA Tour, and he's one of the few lefties. The University of Georgia alum is in his prime, and we should anticipate another solid performance in the 2018 season. In 2017, he played in 30 events and finished in the top 10 in almost half of those. He's already earned bragging rights by having two holes in one (aces) in the same round, one of only three players in PGA history to achieve the feat. Shall we unofficially give Brian the nickname Ace? Jim Carrey fans should approve.

Brian "Ace" Harman 5'7", 154 lbs

Career PGA accolades for Harman include:

- PGA Tour victories: 2

- 2017 FedEx Cup rank: 7

- 2017 U.S. Open: 2nd place (tie)

While James Barry "Jbe'" Kruger[28] doesn't play on the PGA, I thought it would be good to highlight him. He is a professional, and he has won multiple tournaments. He currently plays on the European Tour, Sunshine Tour (Australia), and the Asian Tour. Sources list him from 5'3½" to 5'5". For extra bragging rights, let's go with bigger vertical challenge.

James Barry "Jbe'" Kruger 5'3½", 135 lbs

Tour wins:

- European Tour: 1

- Asian Tour: 1

- Sunshine Tour: 4

Kruger's father was a marathon runner who promised Kruger the opportunity to play pro golf, but only if he became a scratch player by the age of eighteen. Kruger answered the call and went pro. Fittingly,

South African legend Gary Player was his idol, given the two had similar physiques. Kruger faced his fair share of critics and doubters. He embraces them.

"There are good factors in being the smallest ... I think guys definitely underestimate me when they see me. But after my first shot, they don't."

~Jbe' Kruger

Way to go, Jbe'! Drive for show *and* putt for dough.

To recap, if we rank the six major U.S. sports leagues from a percentage of players under 5"10", they are as follows:

1. MLS 29.7%

2. PGA 19.5%

3. NFL 5.3%

4. MLB 4.6%

5. NHL 3.2%

6. NBA 0.5%

If we look at the total number of players per league, the ranks are as follows:

1. MLS 150

2. NFL 90

3. MLB 40

4. NHL 28

5. PGA 18

6. NBA 2

There are other sports to consider; however, this cut covers the major professional sports in the U.S. That said, if you love horses and the sport of horse racing, height bias is just as prevalent there as in the NBA, only perhaps more so, and in our favor. Jockeys tend to be 4'10" to 5'6" and weigh a buck and change. Smaller guys rule the domain of horse racing, hands down. Giddy up. Having not been around horses most of my life, I won't claim to be a horse guy or a cowboy. However, I know people that own horses and others that watch horse racing religiously. Both camps love their respective horses. Saddle up as you see fit.

Chapter-11

Corporate World

The ability to provide leadership and drive enterprise business performance are standard qualifications people look for in a CEO. However, if you recall the topics of heuristics and hardwiring of the brain outlined in the introduction, you may remember that height also plays a factor. Malcolm Gladwell's book *Blink* examines:

> *"In the U.S. population, about 14.5% of all men are six feet or over. Among CEOs of Fortune 500 companies, that number is 58%. Even more strikingly, in the general American population, 3.9% of adult men are 6'2" or taller."*[29]

I think this gives some merit to the saying that some people are natural-born leaders, at least the ones who are six feet tall. Statistics tell us that if two equally qualified men are interviewing for a CEO role and one is vertically challenged while the other is vertically gifted, you can place your bets on the latter.

In his article, "Why Short People Make Better Entrepreneurs," John Warrillow (who is 5'9") collected height data on CEOs and discovered findings similar to Gladwell's. While working in broadcasting, Warrillow claims he faced heightism, which helped push him to launch his own business-to-business (B2B) company. Here are Warrillow's thoughts of why vertically challenged guys rock the startup world:

"Doing versus leading - I think entrepreneurship is an ideal career choice for people who do not have the physical characteristics of leadership. If you're short (or fat or skinny or have funny hair or weird teeth), company building is an ideal career. When you start a business, you're not leading anyone. You're trying to refine a concept, and a premium is placed on ideas, intelligence, and tenacity. It doesn't matter how physically commanding you are, because there's nobody to command.

As your business grows, you may find yourself leading a few dozen people, but even so, a small entrepreneurial company doesn't need a figurehead perched on a pedestal.

By contrast, the job of running a Fortune 500 company, many of which employ more than 100,000 people, is much more about communicating a vision, inspiring your senior people to lead their teams, rallying the troops, persuading regulators to side with you, and being the public face of your company to the media. In short, optics matter more than they do in a startup.

If you're short, fear not. While you may have an uphill battle for the corner office of a big company, you're the perfect height to start your own."
30

If you recall in the introduction, we discussed the brain's preloaded software for making snap decisions, known as heuristics or cognitive bias. In *Blink,* Malcolm Gladwell refers to this as *bad rapid cognition*—in the case of height bias, those first few seconds of meeting a tall person make us predisposed toward thinking of that person as an effective leader. With our subconscious mind at work, taller figures become appealing when it comes to leadership or figures of authority, such as a president or CEO.

How about the impact of height on income? Do taller guys make more money? A study in the *Journal of Applied Psychology,* Standing Tall Pays Off,[31] confirms that an extra inch of height can equate to roughly an extra $800 a year. The study controlled for education and experience, which of course have an impact. The net result: If you're six feet tall, you probably earn about $4,000 more than the equally qualified guy who's in the five-seven club. Over a 40 year career, this equates to $160,000. Not an insignificant chunk of coin. But wait, before we yell "injustice!" and run to the HR manager, let's peel another layer of the onion.

Consider work published in the *Journal of Political Economy:* "The Effect of Adolescent Experience on Labor Market Outcomes:

The Case of Height."[32] The research highlights how height during adolescence, say around age sixteen, impacts self-esteem, which ultimately impacts wages as an adult. The study concludes that self-esteem, once learned, lasts a lifetime. So, if a kid is undersized at age sixteen and develops low self-esteem, even if he sprouts to six-foot status, low self-esteem may still be ingrained. On the flip side, a kid who just stops growing at sixteen but is of average height will likely carry higher self-esteem. Make sense? For any parent who wants their kid to participate in more activities, consider the following excerpt from the study:

"[After] controlling for age, height, region and family background, participation in athletics is associated with an 11.4 percent increase in adult wages, and participation in every club other than athletics is associated with a 5.1 percent increase in wages."

So, if you're on the taller side of the spectrum around adolescence and you're active in sports or clubs, that mitigates the impact of this $1,000-per-inch study. At the opposite side of the spectrum, if a kid is vertically challenged during adolescence and is not participating in group activities, they may be getting short-changed down the road.

I'm sure some of you are thinking: *this isn't exactly motivating. How about some of our crew making it to the top of the proverbial corporate ladder?* If you recall from the introduction, I alluded to the fact our fraternity includes digital juggernauts. We will look at three individuals in the technology sector who've already reached amazing heights and are poised for greater things to come. I'd wager that these are three companies you engage with monthly, weekly, or even hourly. The next time you Google something, "like" your buddy's Facebook post, or buy something on Amazon, know that the respective founders for each company are part of our elite club.

- Sergey Brin, 5'8", co-founder, Google

- Mark Zuckerberg, 5'7", founder and CEO, Facebook

- Jeff Bezos, 5'7", founder and CEO, Amazon

In the digital era, Google, Facebook, and Amazon are three of the most powerful companies on the planet, which by default makes these guys three of the most powerful people on the planet. How's that for club membership?

Jeff Bezos,[33] founder and CEO of Amazon, stands 5'7" and boasts a net worth, as of December 2017, of $97 billion. Bezos graduated from Princeton with a degree in computer science and electrical engineering. He initially entered the financial world, working with a quantitative hedge fund. He attained a VP role but chose to leave the company so he could sell books online. At the time, many people thought this move was crazy, given Bezos's trajectory on Wall Street. However, if we look closer, the move makes a lot of sense. Bezos had a love for reading and technology, and here's his perspective when it comes to decision-making: "We all get to choose our life stories. It's our choices that define us, not our gifts. You can only be proud of your choices," Jeff says. In his words, you either choose a life of "ease and comfort," or of "service and adventure," and he believes when you're 80 [years old], you'll be more proud of the latter.[34]

After reviewing Bezos's interviews with a few of the major tech publications and clips on YouTube, I realized he's pretty consistent with his messaging and words of wisdom. My two biggest takeaways are that he takes a long-term view when making big decisions, and he isn't afraid to make bold moves—he believes that risk is a necessary component of progress. The next time we have a game-changing event knock on our door, let's utilize Bezos's perspective. What would our eighty-year-old selves do? Would we regret doing or *not doing* something? More times than not, I've found, it's the things we don't do that we regret.

As we'll see with other guys who are hitting home runs, Bezos has had more than a few whiffs at the plate. He's candidly stated that his company has invested billions in failed projects. One that comes to mind is the Amazon Fire Phone. Launched in 2014,[35] the phone had some interesting features, such as 3D views and four cameras. However, it never became an Android- or iPhone-killer and was discontinued after less than two years in the market. This came after several years invested in planning and development. Instead of calling it a failure, Bezos and company likely view this as a learning experience. Stay tuned for part II: I anticipate Amazon's next swing at a smartphone will be a four-bagger.

"One of my jobs as the leader of Amazon is to encourage people to be bold."

~ Jeff Bezos

Regarding role models, Bezos believes parents and grandparents can provide great life lessons. Even if his grandfather didn't have the right tools for a job, he had the ingenuity to get it done. Meanwhile, Thomas Edison and Walt Disney were his autobiographical heroes growing up. As inventors and pioneers, Disney execs had a big vision, but they required teams to accomplish the vision. No single person could do it. Edison was the opposite, the inventor who worked solo in his laboratory. Many times we hear childhood stories about high-flying entrepreneurs and CEOs running lemonade stands, trading baseball cards, or scalping concert tickets. The founder of Amazon was different. He was the kid in the garage putting together machines and playing scientist. Today, he is a tech titan who has built a multifaceted company in ecommerce, advertising, streaming video, and web infrastructure services. I'd anticipate he will be listed as the richest person in the world by the time this book is published, surpassing $100 billion in net worth.

Speaking of net worth, perhaps you've heard of this little company called Facebook? Yes, Mark Zuckerberg, the founder and CEO of a social media platform that reaches two billion people on planet Earth, stands all of 5'7". Between me, Bezos, and Zuckerberg, it would be a five-seven convention. And while Zuckerberg has established himself as a social media icon, having a net worth of $73 billion as of December 2017, he reportedly does at least a few things to maximize his height. According to a 2010 *New Yorker* article,[36] he's "only around five feet eight, but he seems taller, because he stands with his chest out and his back straight, as if held up by a string." The author went on to suggest Zuckerberg uses optical illusion to his benefit via staging photos to exaggerate his height, such as being closer to the camera compared to others who may be taller. Interesting that even one of the most successful people on the planet is impacted by height bias. It's OK, Mark, you're in good company, and you can be part of our brotherhood for the vertically challenged.

Last but not least, Google has a member of our club. Co-founder Sergey Brin is 5'8" and has a net worth of over $47 billion. Born in Russia, his family immigrated to the U.S. to escape persecution. With a mathematics and computer science undergrad degree in hand, he went to grad school at Stanford, where the Google bromance would begin with co-founder Larry Page.[37]

This quote from Brin dovetails with a few we've seen:

"The only way you are going to have success is to have lots of failures first."

~ Sergey Brin

The takeaway here of not being afraid of failures—we'll call them *learning opportunities*—could be applied to just about any aspect of life. As for another theme we've seen, consider the following:

"Coming up with an idea is the least important part of creating something great. It has to be the right idea and have good taste, but the execution and delivery are what's key."

~ Sergey Brin

Ideas are good, but they are useless unless you take action.

In addition to being under 5'10" and ridiculously wealthy tech titans, Bezos, Zuckerberg, and Brin have another thing in common: they are all entrepreneurs. This isn't to say that you can't work for a company and climb the corporate ladder; however, if you hit a glass ceiling, it may be worthwhile to consider if heightism or height bias exists in your organization. Jack Welch, the legendary former CEO of GE (General Electric), stood just 5'7" but managed to climb the ranks and improve the company's value 4,000% during his twenty-year CEO tenure.[38] Not too shabby.

If you buy into the notion that the advent of the Internet and digital technologies have "flattened" the world as in Thomas Friedman's book *The World is Flat,* then it isn't a stretch to embrace a similar mindset of digital platforms leveling the playing field with regards to height. Yes, you may be short in photos (though do remember previous tips on distance from the camera, and taller people). However in the realm of email, social media, and other digital channels, even the most vertically challenged guy can become a digital giant. Throughout my professional career, I've benefited from the global reach of LinkedIn, Twitter, and to a lesser extent, Facebook. The power of the network effect is pretty amazing. You're closer than you think to connecting with just about anyone in the world.

If you've read his books or listened to Tim Ferriss's podcasts, you know he is a towering figure in entrepreneurship and self-improvement. Originally focused on the business and tech start-up arena, the five-foot-nine Ferriss now makes his mark by interviewing the best of the best across a wide variety of disciplines. In addition to insightful podcasts, Ferriss is the author of New York Times bestseller 4-Hour Work Week and a handful of other books. He's provided me with new ways to view how the business world works as well as the mindset to continually experiment, question the status quo, and challenge myself. Another educational and inspiring podcast for the business-minded is John Lee Dumas's *Entrepreneur on Fire.* Dumas focuses on productivity and organization—two areas that are critical if you ever want to publish a book, I've discovered.

Now, perhaps you're already interested or passionate about a certain area, such as technology. If so, I'd say run with it and follow your passion. Perhaps understanding business and financials is your jam—that's great as well. If you are still searching for that "one thing," fear not. Many people, myself included, spend years trying to figure out what makes themselves tick. You may uncover multiple things that inspire you, and that's cool too. There are plenty of people who have "slash" careers, the accountant that also has a woodworking business, or the firefighter who teaches self-improvement, like my buddy Jake Nawrocki. His *Operation Self Reset* podcasts[2] provided some tools which helped me push through limiting beliefs while training for my last big Spartan race.

Throughout my professional career, I've always appreciated the power of written words. A well-crafted letter, email, or tweet can serve as a springboard to meeting people and having conversations that otherwise would never happen. Initially, I found a voice writing short stories in grade school, winning a young authors award; this happened even though I was a fifth grader competing with sixth graders. Later, I found the power of the digital pen (email), which helped me in sales and business development. It's invaluable to be succinct in writing to potential clients, mitigating fire drills, and creating compelling

---

[2] http://operationselfreset.com/podcasts/

outreach for executives who receive hundreds of emails from vendors trying to peddle their goods.

When I wrote reports analyzing the business strategies of Facebook, Google, Adobe, IBM, and Microsoft, the vast majority of my clients didn't know my height. We knew each other only virtually, and suffice to say, they didn't care how tall I was. They wanted to know who was winning or losing and the next moves of these IT market makers. What really mattered was that I took pride in my work and applied myself each day to deliver value to my clients.

Chapter-12

Government and Politics

I was amazed to find out an icon of the American civil rights movement of the 1950s and 1960s would qualify as vertically challenged. This same gentleman won the Nobel Peace Prize in 1964.

Dr. Martin Luther King, Jr. was all of 5'7", yet he had the courage to stand against discrimination and adversity most of us will never know, advocating equal rights for all. He dedicated his life to ensuring people would be treated the same way in this country, regardless of their ethnicity, religion, or sex. Height discrimination was likely not something he considered at the time, but I believe Dr. King would approve of this endeavor to help vertically challenged guys get a fair shake. Anyone who has watched, listened, or read Dr. King's work can feel his passion. His oratory skills are amazing, such that I had no idea how tall he was until I began this book. He was always larger than life in my mind.

Standard history books and classes are not likely to highlight Dr. King's height. Keep him in mind the next time you're facing scrutiny or bias based on your height, or if you're struggling with any difficult situation, for that matter. Have the courage to stand up for yourself or others peacefully.

Another man who would qualify for our fraternity could be viewed as a hybrid, given his accomplishments in the business world and politics. Michael Bloomberg served as New York City mayor for an unprecedented three terms. Prior to serving as mayor, Bloomberg developed Windows-based software in the 1980s which continues to power a significant portion of today's financial sector. Bloomberg is all of 5'8", but has climbed to be the seventh richest person in the United States and the tenth-richest globally. As of January 2018, he has an estimated net worth of over $50 billion. In addition to being a business mogul and politician, Bloomberg is a philanthropist. A member of The Giving Pledge, a group of billionaires who promise to donate at least half of their wealth to philanthropies either directly, or through a will. There are no height limitations when it comes to charitable causes.

There is plenty of what I'll label as misinformation flying around claiming that the taller U.S. presidential candidate always wins, or has won since the turn of the century. Neither of these statements are accurate. The fourth president of the United States, James Madison, is known as the "Father of the Constitution," given that he wrote the initial drafts. He also sponsored the Bill of Rights. Neither of these would have been possible if he wasn't confident:

"The circulation of confidence is better than the circulation of money."

~ James Madison

Regarded as a small, quiet intellectual, Madison leveraged knowledge across a number of disciplines. His knowledge gave him confidence. Power and leadership followed. People believed in Madison to the point they entrusted him with helping form a new type of government. His thoughts and ideas provided the framework that shaped this nation.[39] If we use today's 5'10" benchmark for height, Madison is the most vertically challenged president in history at 5'6". In 1808, when Madison's presidency started, the average height for males was 5'7", so he wasn't that much below average. However, he did beat out a taller opponent: Charles C. Pinckney was 5'9".

Chapter-13

Military and National Aeronautics and Space Administration (NASA)

In the past, height discrimination prevented vertically challenged guys from serving in this country's military. It took one of America's biggest heroes during World War II to open the door for the undersized. Audie Murphy was rejected by the military multiple times, but he was determined to serve his country. You are about to read about one of the few real-life superheroes. Understandably, his plot is one of the most frequently visited at Arlington National Cemetery.

Texas native Audie Murphy was 5'5" and was told he was too small to join the Marines or be a paratrooper. He was also too young, but he somehow navigated around that. Through perseverance, Murphy would eventually join the U.S. Army, rising to the rank of lieutenant. Later he would join the National Guard in his home state.

Audie Murphy, 5'5", Lieutenant, U.S. Army; Major, U.S. National Guard, 112 lbs

During WWII, Murphy fought in nine campaigns and was wounded three times. His courage earned him thirty-three awards. This includes honors from the United States, as well as France and Belgium.

A list of Murphy's accolades include:

- Medal of Honor (1945)

- Distinguished Service Cross (1944)

- 2 Silver Stars (1944)

- Legion of Merit (1945)

- 2 Bronze Stars (1945 – included valor for service; 1954)

- 3 Purple Hearts (1944 – twice, 1945)

- French Legion of Honor, Grade of Chevalier (1945)

- Belgian Croix de Guerre with Palm (1945)

- Outstanding Civilian Service Medal (1961)

- Texas Legislative Medal of Honor (2013)

During a tank fight in Holtzwihr, France, in January 1945, one of the men in Murphy's unit recalled his actions:

"For an hour he held off the enemy force single-handed, fighting against impossible odds ... [the] greatest display of guts and courage I have ever seen."

~ Private Anthony Abramski

According to additional sources[3] that recalled the event in detail, Murphy climbed atop a burning enemy tank and proceeded to unleash its .50 caliber on six German tanks and 250 German infantry. This held the German forces at bay, while allowing his unit to retreat. We thank you for your service, Lieutenant Murphy.

In addition to his military accomplishments, Murphy was also a poet, actor, and movie producer. Audie's movies, such as the WWII-era autobiography *To Hell and Back,* won him a place on the Hollywood Walk of Fame (star #1558). All of these accomplishments are even more impressive if we consider that his father left the family when he was just fifteen years old, and his mother would die the following year. Only sixteen and no parents? I can't imagine. These hardships likely galvanized an already strong-minded kid, helping prepare him for the war and to do heroic things. If you are looking for a confidence builder, consider the following words from this war hero:

---

[3] http://www.historynet.com/audie-murphy-one-man-stand-at-holtzwihr.htm

"[If] you're scared of something you'd better get busy and do something about it. I'd call that a challenge – and I believe that the way to grow is to meet all the challenges as they come along."

~ Audie Murphy

Each time we overcome challenges or adversity, we grow. Some are huge life-altering events, others are the smaller but more frequent speed bumps we all face in life.

You may be curious what the average height is for today's service members. I found limited data, except for the Navy Seals,[4] who are on average 5'10" and 175 lbs. USMC.net,[5] a resource for information about the Marines, addresses the question: *how big are Marines?*

When many people think of Marines, they often picture buffed out men standing over six feet tall, and swaggering around like John Wayne. However, other than the basic height requirement, size has absolutely nothing to do with how good or gifted or talented a Marine can be. Ask anyone who has been to any military training program or special forces training program, and they will tell you that what matters most of all is spirit, mental discipline, determination, and a desire to excel.

---

[4]   https://www.quora.com/Who-would-win-in-a-heads-up-hand-to-hand-battle-32-NFL-running-backs-or-32-Navy-seals

[5] https://www.usmc.net/how_big_are_marines/

Throughout the history of the United States Marine Corps, famous Marines have come in all shapes and sizes. While the majority of Marines are in good physical condition, height has nothing to do with intelligence or the ability to get a job done. Don't let anyone ever tell you that brawn is more important than brains, because it just isn't true.

From my seat, serving one's country is extremely admirable. I am proud that one of my "circle of five" friends who is a Marine (even when not active duty, a Marine is always a Marine) also happens to be part of the vertically challenged club. He is one of the most accomplished, intelligent, confident, and charismatic people I know. He embraces his intangibles to make an impression and do good. From my perspective, he has done well in just about every aspect of life: he's educated, a family guy, a world traveler, an entrepreneur, a black belt in martial arts, and he defended our country during a major conflict. He reconfirmed that in addition to loving a guy in uniform, many women appreciate a sense of humor, especially his voices of different cartoon characters and personas. War is no laughing matter; however, there is a time and a place for everything. Stay funny, my friends.

The next time you look to the stars, know that multiple guys from our fraternity have been crews on missions for the National Aeronautics and Space Administration (NASA). NASA's vision: *We reach for new heights and reveal the unknown for the benefit of humankind.* Believe it or not, President Eisenhower set the height limit of the crew for the first space mission at 5'11". This was due to the tight quarters within the spacecraft. This set the stage for multiple members of the Original Seven being under 5'10". We'll review the most vertically challenged, the one who reached amazing heights, literally and figuratively.

Gus Grissom was highly decorated as both a pilot in the Air Force and as an astronaut with NASA. He attained the ranking of lieutenant in the Air Force and was a crew member on three NASA missions. Grissom was the second American to fly in space and the first person to fly in space twice. He was a member of the Original Seven crew and piloted the Liberty Bell 7 spacecraft. Grissom was 5'5", and a bio on NASA's website reads as follows:

Although Grissom was too short to participate in high school sports, he found a niche for himself in the local Boy Scout troop where he eventually served as leader of the Honor Guard. To earn spending money, he delivered newspapers twice a day throughout the year and, in the summer, he was hired by the local growers to pick peaches and cherries in the orchards outside of town.

Grissom was, in his own words "not much of a whiz in school". Without having set specific goals for himself, he simply seemed to drift through his classes. He excelled in math, but only pulled average grades in his other subjects. His high school principal remembered him as "an average solid citizen who studied just about enough to get a diploma."

118

OK, so far Grissom sounds like a fairly average guy who is punching up given his height. He would soon take a more active role in determining his path in life:

> [W]orld War II helped Grissom start forming some personal and career goals. He enlisted as an aviation cadet as a high school senior and reported for duty in August 1944 following graduation . . . he had high hopes of . . . flying combat missions. However, Japan surrendered a short time later and the war ended before he could receive his training. Grissom found himself going from one routine desk job to another. Knowing that he had joined the Air Force to fly and not to type, he decided to leave the service. His discharge came through in November 1945.

> Grissom soon realized that his limited military career was going to get him nowhere. Eventually, he found a job at Carpenter's Bus Body Works. However, he knew that he did not want to spend the rest of his life installing doors on school buses. Therefore, he set another goal for himself. He would earn a bachelor's degree in mechanical engineering from Purdue University.

Do you see the adjustment in Grissom's plan of action? He hit the proverbial wall and recalibrated. By managing the situation, he would set himself up for achieving his goal of being a fighter pilot and more. Gus flipped burgers at night and took classes during the day. He found it difficult to find employment, largely because he still wanted to be a test pilot. Following his passion, he would re-enlist in the Air Force and finish air cadet training, earning wings as a pilot. Within the year, Grissom would be shipped out to fight in the Korean War. His contributions included flying over one hundred missions in only six months. He requested more missions, but the country decided he had done his part and wanted to welcome him home. We thank you for your service, Gus.

Virgil Ivan "Gus" Grissom, Lieutenant Colonel, U.S. Air Force, 5'5"

- Air Force Command Astronaut Wings
- Distinguished Flying Cross
- Air Medal with Cluster
- Congressional Space Medal of Honor
- NASA Distinguished Service Medal (awarded twice)
- American Campaign Medal
- World War II Victory Medal
- Korean Service Medal (with two stars)
- United Nations Korea Medal
- Korean War Service Medal

Given his accomplishments, Grissom was slated as commander of Apollo 1, the spaceship for the first Earth-orbit mission, the ship that would take man to the moon. However, in a prelaunch training session, a fire would kill Grissom and crew members Ed White and Roger Chaffee. There is speculation that Grissom was in line to be the first man to walk on the moon.

As a fighter pilot and astronaut, you'd think Grissom was born with ice water in his veins. However, during post-landing conferences and subsequent interviews, he admitted that there were times he was scared. It's OK to accept fear; what's more important is having the courage to take action. We'll close with a quote from the war hero and astronaut:

"If we die, we want people to accept it. We're in a risky business, and we hope that if anything happens to us it will not delay the program. The conquest of space is worth the risk of life."

~ Virgil "Gus" Grissom

Chapter-14

Music and Entertainment

In her book *Shortchanged: Height Discrimination and Strategies for Social Change,* author and lawyer Tanya Osensky discusses height bias. I was amazed at one passage from Osensky's book where she compiled a list of short characters in television shows and movies. She points out that shorter guys are usually relegated to the role of the taller character's friend or sidekick, such as Tonto to the Lone Ranger, Barney Rubble to Fred Flintstone, Robin to Batman, and George Costanza to Jerry Seinfeld. I'll peel this onion another layer, going back to the notion of taller people being more intelligent: Tonto means "foolish" in Spanish. Not nice.

Osensky casts a particularly harsh light on the movie *Captain America.* The main character is a wimpy 5'4" kid who, after participating in a lab experiment, becomes our hero at 6'2".

I'll provide an alternative view. Ironically, the same society that places us in supporting roles or pokes fun of the vertically challenged will also root for the vertically challenged. Support may come directly or indirectly, secretly or publicly. How can this be? Pulling for the smaller guy is ingrained through children's books, cartoons, and movies. Think back to *The Little Engine that Could, Mighty Mouse, Underdog,* or *Rudy.* In the movie *Star Wars,* hero Luke Skywalker is a little short for a stormtrooper but through proper training and determination, becomes one of the most powerful Jedi Knights in the galaxy.

The entertainment industry is massive and provides a wide array of opportunities for people of various heights.

For example, day or night, Ryan Seacrest has become a media icon. He hosts the morning talk show *Live with Kelly and Ryan* as well as *American Idol.* These shows are watched by millions. While women—and let's be honest, a lot of men—consider Seacrest a handsome guy, he wasn't exactly a heartthrob growing up. In addition to wearing braces and glasses, he was a chunky kid, teased by classmates. We see a guy on stage who is arguably the best of the best, filled with confidence and charisma. However, were you aware Seacrest is only 5'7"? If he didn't take pride in living a healthy lifestyle, he likely would not have risen to stardom.

In an interview with *Men's Health* magazine, Seacrest discusses the benefits of putting down the extra cookies and nachos, opting for a more healthy lifestyle:

"I know it gave me a little bit of confidence where, maybe, I didn't have it before. It gave me some satisfaction to put on a pair of pants and feel good in them. It felt great and allowed me to walk into a room and feel less self-conscious. So, yes, I'd say it allowed me to build some confidence early on. I remember both feelings; I remember not having the confidence and then gaining it and going through that transformation. I haven't forgotten about that."

People will talk about how superficial it is to judge people based on their appearance, but this is how much of society operates. Short guys may not be able to control height, but we can maximize our appearance by eating healthy and working out. Being the short guy is one thing, but being the short *and overweight* guy is another.

Let's jump back to the interview.

Men's Health: What's your best advice, based on everything you've been through?

"I think balance is important for all of us, physically and emotionally. It's tough, it's not easy to do, but I do think we strive for balance in our lives. That's balancing your career, balancing your diet, and balancing your family. That would be my advice, because it's what I try to focus on—but even I don't always achieve it."

Many people, myself included, can become hyper-focused on a particular area of life, and neglect other areas. For example, periodic moonlighting or working a few weekends on a side hustle project, such as a self-help book, is reasonable and kept me mostly in balance. Repeatedly shutting out friends and family for weeks or months could be viewed as an unhealthy situation, however.

Before we close, it's worth noting that on the *Ryan and Kelly* Show, Mr. Seacrest replaced Michael Strahan, a 6'5" former NFL defensive end for the New York Giants. Unlike the famous "next man up" motto used by the New England Patriots, whereby a player of similar stature will fill an open position, the entertainment industry tends to have a mindset that talent, in this case charisma and likability, supersede any type of height requirement.

If we look at movies, TV, music, and comedy, we find plenty of smaller guys doing big things. Movies such as *Iron Man, Top Gun,* and *Lord of the Rings* star Robert Downey Jr. at 5'9", Tom Cruise at 5'8", and Elijah Wood at 5'6", respectively. Meanwhile, former TV talk show icon Jon Stewart of *The Daily Show* is 5'6". The hits don't stop here as rapper Pitbull rocks the world at 5'7", and the multifaceted musician, singer, and songwriter Bruno Mars is all of 5'5". Going back in time, Michael J. Fox is 5'4", while *The Godfather* star Al Pacino is 5'7". For you card sharks, Dustin Hoffman is 5'6" and provides a one-two combo in *Rain Man* with Tom Cruise. How's that for a cast of vertically challenged amazingness?

If we look back at the history of music, the 5'7" Bob Dylan achieved amazing heights with a career spanning five decades. Britannica.com provides a glimpse into the folk legend's bio:

"He personified a new form of American music in the mid-1960s. Dylan brought together the amplified beat of rock and roll, the star imagery of pop, the historical and political sensibility of folk, and—through the wit, ambition, and obscurity of his lyrics—the arrogance of urban bohemia. He gave the emerging rock scene artistic weight (his was album, not Top 40, music) and a new account of youth as an ideological rather than a demographic category."[40]

A list of Dylan's accolades include:

- 10 Grammies, 38 Grammy nominations

- Golden Globe (2001)

- Nobel Prize in Literature (2016)

"Gonna change my way of thinking, make myself a different set of rules. Gonna put my good foot forward and stop being influenced by fools."

~ Bob Dylan

Dylan was labelled by many as a non-conformist; others would say a trailblazer or even a rebel. Regardless, he had the courage to follow his heart and stand tall. He infuriated even his fans by using electric instruments, which was taboo for his genre at the time.

As we've seen, society may be biased about height, but it appreciates entertainment from people of all walks of life, short guys included. As a comedy fan, the only really tall comedian I can think of is Jim Carrey, who stands 6'2". Perhaps taller guys subscribe to playing it cool, and humor isn't part of their program? Just a thought. On the flip side, Aziz Ansari is 5'6", and the late Robin Williams stood 5'7". When we aren't being made fun of, we can make funny. Or something like that. OK, let's get back on track before you start throwing tomatoes at me.

Kevin Hart is an actor, producer, and comedian. He also happens to be 5'4". Hart holds the distinct record for performing in front of the largest sellout crowd for a comedy show in the U.S. Typically, larger comedy shows will be in the 10,000-plus attendance range. In 2015, Hart headlined a sellout show at Lincoln Financial Field in Philadelphia to the tune of 50,000 people.[41] If you watch this show on Netflix, you'll see him perform a James Bond skit, and instead of Agent 007, Hart opts to be Agent 054. Is it a coincidence these numbers align with his height? I think not. Way to own it, Kevin.

As with other high achievers, Hart's career included some major hurdles. Initially, he tried performing at comedy shows and open mics and was not successful. Hart chalks this up to not really understanding who he was or what content to use. Fortunately Hart found a mentor, Keith Robinson, who helped him ditch styles and material he was repurposing from other comics. Armed with his own style and content from his real life experiences, success would follow. So how does one of the most vertically challenged guys make it to the biggest of stages? His advice is as follows:

The best tip I could tell you is to be active. So many people talk about what they want to do and they just love words. Put actions behind your words. Don't be a talker, be a doer.

~ Kevin Hart

There you go. Talking the talk is easy; taking action is where the magic happens. It's so easy to keep the same mindset you've always had; however, if you're seeking change, follow Hart's advice and be a doer. Get after it. After writing hundreds of commentaries and reports on enterprise IT and digital advertising, I decided it was time to write a book on a completely different subject. The content certainly didn't flow like water. It required countless hours researching, writing, and revising … and probably needs more fine-tuning. But as Facebook's Mark Zuckerberg famously said, *"Done is better than perfect."*

Chapter-15

Growth Through Adversity

Most of us are fortunate enough to grow up in households where we have access to ample food, a warm bed, and other comforts. Other people, though, are not afforded these luxuries that are too often taken for granted. Imagine growing up in the ghetto of Grand Rapids, Michigan where gunshots and drug deals were commonplace. Imagine your house didn't have heat or electricity. Imagine at the age of one, you were used as a human shield during a family dispute that included a gun. This was the household environment in which professional fighter Floyd Mayweather Jr. was raised. At 5'8", Mayweather is known as one of the best boxers in the history of the sport. To say he grew up in adverse conditions would be putting it mildly. In an interview, Mayweather provided a glimpse into the tough love he received growing up: *"I got whippings all the time, my father would beat me for anything I did, even if I hadn't done*

anything. I used to pray for the day I could become an adult and get away from it. I got tired of getting beat."[42]

While Mayweather certainly didn't exactly enter a profession that precluded him from getting beat, he is consistently noted as a superb defensive fighter. His record of 50-0 is the best boxing record of all time, and he is the first boxer to hold the title in five different weight classes. Nicknamed "Money" for not being afraid to flaunt his bankroll, Mayweather has earned an estimated $700 million during his career. However, before he became rich, he fought in over 100 matches as an amateur. This makes that summer internship without pay seem a little less cruel, right? As he rose through the ranks, Mayweather demonstrated a high level of talent and commitment, winning 84 of 102 matches. This formula allowed him to maximize his performance. Height has never been a focal point for the boxing icon. Instead, he focused on fine-tuning his craft and mindset, stating, "You have good days, you have bad days. But the main thing is to grow mentally." Whether you are a boxing fan or rooted for Money during any of his bouts, his ability to overcome adversity and rise up are truly amazing.

Little guys get picked on by bigger guys every day. Initially I thought dedicating part of a chapter to bullies would be beneficial for teenagers or tweens, but certainly bullying happens in the adult world, too. Yes, adult bullies exist—they're usually the same young bullies, but older. Even after the days of recess are long gone, bullies continue

132

to flex on those who they deem physically inferior. Typical targets include the vertically challenged.

Facebook, Twitter, and Snapchat did not exist during my school years. As someone who analyzes the businesses of these companies, I am aware they wield significant power in society—and it's not always used for the greater good. As major news outlets and documentaries continue to highlight, social media can drain productivity and ironically can actually impede social interaction. Social media also serve as platforms for bullies to unleash psychological warfare. Many times the digital damage inflicted will be more of a factor than actual physical intimidation. In her book *Shortchanged: Height Discrimination and Strategies for Social Change,* Tanya Osensky highlights the wide ranging impact teasing and social pressures can have on victims and their parents.

Fortunately my interactions with bullies were limited to my school-age years, and only a couple of altercations come to mind. Coincidentally, both instances included being whitewashed (for you warm-weather people, this is having your face rubbed in the snow). On one occasion, an upperclassman introduced my face to a snowbank and then delivered an epic wedgie in front of my buddies. Fortunately my braces didn't cut my mouth, and perhaps the ice and snow provided some exfoliation benefits to my pimply complexion at the time. This type of event isn't on par with getting mocked in front of the entire school or digital world through social media, but it certainly wasn't a confidence booster.

If you are a teenager, hopefully you don't have to worry about bullies. But perhaps you become a target of bullies at school, or one of your friends is? What do you do? If you're an adult, you may not be at risk of a wedgie, but situations will still occur periodically.

Unfortunately, undersized individuals tend to be the least likely to raise their hands or reach out to a parent, a teacher, or a coach when being bullied. Bullied kids may be quiet or shy. Add to this the belief that society tells us that asking for help is a sign of weakness, and that further compounds the matter. There's a reason boxers and UFC fighters have weight classes. While height isn't directly proportional to weight, height does have a significant impact on weight. Bigger guys have the upper hand when it comes to physical altercations. As adults, we can typically diffuse situations, but under some circumstances, you may need to defend yourself or others. Martial arts teaches self-defense, but there are other benefits. In my experience, studying martial arts is great for discipline, self-confidence, and conditioning, both physical and mental.

For those who've seen the movie *The Karate Kid,* Ralph Macchio is the new kid in town who gets picked on by a ruthless gang of karate-infused bullies, known as the Cobra Kai. Macchio befriends Mr. Miyagi, who becomes his sensei. After training and more than a few life lessons, Ralph takes down the Cobra Kai gang who harass and bully him. He also wins the girl. Score another for the underdog, right? Yes, however, our hero also repeatedly gets his butt kicked, so don't go trying the crane kick on some bigger dude just because he's picking on you at recess. Even the mighty Bruce Lee believed the best fight was the one that never happened. Violence is not the answer. An eye for an eye and a tooth for a tooth leaves us all blind, with dentures.

I've shared these anecdotes to bring some lightheartedness to the topic; however, pretending that bullying doesn't exist is almost as bad as resorting to violence. For anyone facing bullies, please know that asking for help doesn't indicate weakness. Rather, it's a sign of intelligence. Concerned what females think about bullies? For each female that likes the bully (who's really a coward), there is another who appreciates the guy who lives by the Golden Rule. In difficult times, find a voice of reason. You may need to look to multiple people to find a solution.

Fortunately, I didn't have to deal with too many bullies, and I wasn't the smallest kid. Ironically, I was considered tall at one point in life. In the sixth grade, I reached my adult height. This placed me on the taller side for a few years. During a routine physical, a doctor informed me and my mom that I would be 6'3". This did not sound crazy, given that was my uncle's height. However, my growth halted, and the promise of being a dual-threat, six-foot-three hoops-and-baseball star faded. For a few years, I thought the height gods had played a cruel trick.

But my height stalling was trivial compared to what would happen my sophomore year of high school. In a car accident, I was ejected from the backseat, landing in the road. The impact resulted in a collapsed lung, shattered pelvis and over thirty stitches in my head. It would take over seven hours for a world-class orthopedic surgeon to piece me back together. A month and a half later, the new me would exit Wentworth-Douglass Hospital with crutches and permanent hardware in the form of a metal plate and several screws, plus a *much* greater appreciation for wearing a seatbelt. The National Highway Traffic Safety Administration reports a survival rate of only 20 percent when passengers are ejected during accidents. So please, buckle those seatbelts.

As an adult, I'd encounter additional speed bumps (no pun intended) for added character-building, coming in the form of thyroid disease and eye disease. These related, yet separate autoimmune disorders are not well understood, each providing a different set of challenges. The butterfly-shaped thyroid gland located at the base of the neck operates much like a thermostat for the body, regulating heart rate and food digestion. An overactive or underactive thyroid can affect energy levels, sleep quality, and the ability to concentrate. In approximately 25 percent of hyperthyroid cases, eye disease occurs. Symptoms typically include swelling of the eye muscles, which causes the eyes to bulge. The eyes themselves may also become bloodshot and irritated.

136

In my situation, I was diagnosed with Graves' Disease, a form of hyperthyroidism. I lost virtually all of my muscle, going from 160 pounds to 130 pounds in about two months. I was sweating constantly, and my heart felt like it was going to jump out of my chest. Just as I was coming to terms with the thyroid situation, symptoms of eye disease emerged. My appearance slowly morphed into that of a frog who'd smoked some good marijuana (not that I know good from bad). The net result would be two surgeries. I revisited my friends at Wentworth-Douglass for a complete thyroidectomy or removal of the thyroid. Three years later, I visited Columbia-Presbyterian Medical Center for a procedure to reduce the orbital swelling that caused my eyes to bulge. While I don't quite look the same as I did prior to eye disease and I need to take daily thyroid medication, I understand the value of good health and self-care.

Despite participating in sports and being an active guy, I've only had one sports-related injury. It was a doozy. During a game in the New York City Urban Professionals Basketball League, I ruptured my Achilles tendon. It was a complete tear and provided a sensation that I will never forget. In the following weeks, I would call upon the crutching skills learned in high school, undergo yet another surgery and begin the recovery process. After one more recreational basketball game, I decided to hang up the high-tops. Since then, I've opted to focus on improving 5K times and weight-training, while exploring new activities, such as yoga and Spartan races.

Sometimes life gives you a slice of humble pie. Sometimes you get a second slice. It may seem like you have been given an entire pie. The mental and physical toughness gained from these types of life-altering events can define us, much more so than our height can.

Maybe you've had a health-related setback, or you've fallen down in another aspect of life. Hey, at least it's easier for us vertically challenged guys to get back up again, right? So, get back on the horse. Even if you don't immediately see the silver lining of a crappy situation today, there will be a time in the not-so-distant future when you look back and see how the experience contributed to your growth as a person. In addition to helping yourself, you can also help others who may take note of your situation and constructive actions. By reading this little memoir, perhaps I motivate someone to wear a seatbelt, and they stay clear of the emergency room.

Many people will have different life chapters and personas as they go through life discovering what makes them tick. For some, the path is easier than for others. For me, the journey has been filled with ups and downs. I've made mistakes and fallen down plenty of times. Learning from mistakes is a good thing. Repeating the same missteps is not.

Sometimes you need to test the water and try out an opportunity before you know for sure if it's a fit. It could be a job, a sport, an instrument—how do you know for sure unless you experience it firsthand? Don't rely on others to decide for you, either directly or indirectly through their height bias or other beliefs. Let the doubters doubt. Even if you don't accomplish exactly what you set out for, new experiences help you grow as a person.

At this stage of my career, I've learned that I enjoy writing, research, and crunching numbers, which made this book a fun project for me. However, this current endeavor actually aligns with an interest in writing that began for me as early as fifth grade. My non-fiction piece didn't make the *New York Times* bestseller list, but *The Island of Savages* won me a Young Author award at Garrison Elementary School. Written in cursive and topped with a colorful cover design, which I also crafted, my tome was a captain's log that detailed an adventure about a shipwreck on a tropical island. At the time, writing wasn't exactly considered "cool" by my circle as compared to sports or video games, which captured most of my time. Being able to identify or hear these positive, supportive signals from areas outside your standard wheelhouse of activities is easier when you make time to reflect, removing chatter from the outside world.

With that said, perhaps through serendipity or some other randomness, you've encountered a similar situation where you inexplicably performed well or enjoyed doing something completely outside your typical comfort zone? Think about it for a bit. You may decide to put down the baseball or shut off the PlayStation and pick up that guitar or that book on Python. The reverse could also be the case. Had I known being a professional video game player was a legit career path, I may have leveraged my citywide credentials as *The Nintendo Kid.*

In order to achieve great heights where you express your talent or passion, it may benefit you to sharpen other areas. For example, like for many people, speaking in front of groups is outside my comfort zone. If I want to continue my pursuit of being a writer and podcaster, a one-two punch of writing and public speaking is hugely valuable. To improve my presentation skills, I joined a local Toastmasters[6] club. If you're not familiar, Toastmasters is an organization that helps people develop public speaking and leadership skills. Squeamish about getting up in front of people or managing things that impact a group? Join the club (no pun intended). Time and time again in life you'll find that you're either *forced* to speak in front of groups or have *opportunities* to speak. Similarly, you'll encounter situations that call for leadership. Your mindset will most likely depend on your skills. Like attaining just about any skill, public speaking takes practice and commitment. I still get those butterflies in my stomach when speaking in front of groups, but they diminish with each repetition. And you don't need to envision yourself as a CEO for leadership skills to be an asset. They can be valuable in coaching, mentoring or guiding others in less formal settings.

---

[6] http://www.toastmasters.org/

Practice isn't fun, but repetitions are the name of the game in acquiring any skill. Much like shooting free throws in hoops, practicing chords on guitar, or memorizing the quadratic formula. If you saw an *All Things Digital* interview[7] of Mark Zuckerberg back in 2010, you felt sorry for the guy. Initially he seemed all cool with his hoodie, but quickly became nervous as the questions begin, sweating and eventually shedding the hoodie despite earlier saying he "never" takes it off. Today, he's much more polished and confident. We can probably attribute this to hours and hours of training and repetitions. So, if you're looking for a way to get an edge in what could easily be considered a valuable lifelong skill, start taking those speaking opportunities. Ask people you consider good speakers for advice or inquire as to how they sharpened their skills.

Many times, people will be more interested in how you say something than what you actually say. Strange but true. So, if you want to command more attention at work or in social settings, public speaking skills are a nice asset to have in your back pocket. As discussed, developing public speaking skills evolves over time. Become a student of the game. During my *Ice Breaker,* the first speech for members of Toastmasters, I didn't exactly feel confidence coursing through my veins. Far from it. However, I felt significantly more comfortable than I would have three months earlier. It still seems a bit

---

[7] http://allthingsd.com/20100602/mark-zuckerberg-session/

ridiculous standing in my living room speaking to an audience of zero, but I understand what's required to reach my goal. Eventually, I will have the skills and confidence to *stand tall* while speaking in front of others. When people in this country are surveyed, they consistently list public speaking as one of their greatest fears.[43] If you're looking to rise above the crowd, public speak skills will help you stand out.

Chapter-16

Health and Fitness

"Take care of your body. It's the only place you can live."

~Jim Rohn

Unlike vertically gifted guys, the vertically challenged are not able to hide weight as easy. When you're already low to the ground, looking wider could be considered a benefit, though. It's all about perspective and strength or fitness goals.

My perspective has been this: if tall, dark, and handsome isn't something I can manage, then I'll focus on taking control of my diet and staying active. And yes, at least Mom says I'm handsome ... but she's biased.

This chapter will be a bit different from the previous as I'll outline the formula for my health. For the past twenty years, I've been a student of the game when it comes to health and nutrition (admittedly better at some times than others), so the learnings and routines are from my playbook. Please check with your doctor before trying out anything that follows.

An active lifestyle has a different meaning, depending on who you ask. For me, weight training and running have been an excellent one-two punch for staying in shape. Add to the mix yoga's benefits, such as flexibility and mental health. Never considered yoga because it's not for guys? Think again. When I lived in NYC, my colleague, who'd also just moved to the city from Colorado, invited me to a yoga class, saying it would be "a life-changing experience." The instructor would make a similar statement, guaranteeing I would return for another class. Nearly a decade later, yoga is part of my daily routine. Oh, and yoga classes aren't bad if you like a 5-to-1 female-to-male ratio (excuse me, where do I sign up?).

This segues into *getting comfortable with the uncomfortable.* Seriously, if you are tired of the small life, why not try new things that can potentially become game changers? Yoga welcomes people of all shapes and sizes. If you asked me ten years ago if I'd ever embrace yoga, I would have laughed. Today I can say that I've met amazing people through yoga, and I've acquired a deeper appreciation for the mind, body, and soul. *Namaste* (rough translation: the light within me honors the light within you). I can tell you're starting to feel enlightened already.

As an adult, I transitioned from high school sports to intramurals to men's leagues. At some point, I joined the ranks of my family and started running, which is largely an individual sport. Perhaps it was for the runner's high and the endorphins, or the fact I couldn't get denied running the local 5K. Despite my appreciation for the sport, I'm the only non-marathoner in my family, and I can say that my mom (all of 5'3") is arguably the best runner and overall athlete in my family. She gets partial credit for my height and full credit for my healthy lifestyle. Known as "Marathon Mary" by her friends, she has run the Boston Marathon nine times. In addition to running strong in her 70s, she's a downhill skier and races competitively, qualifying for a national race where she got to run gates with Olympic Gold Medalist Bode Miller. How cool is that? OK, so Mom isn't part of our fraternity, but the idea here is that the sport of running, like skiing, does not exclude people due to height. You can run anything from 100-meter sprints to ultramarathons. If you are curious, technically any distance greater than 26.2 miles is considered an ultra, but most ultras are 50K (just over 30 miles). If you want to build mental toughness, running is an excellent sport.

While running serves as my platform to build both speed and mental strength, obstacle course races (OCRs) take things to another level—for me, anyhow. Today, OCRs come in a variety of flavors and formats. Two of the more popular are Tough Mudders and Spartan Races. I have competed in about a half-dozen Spartans. In 2017, I completed the trifecta, which is finishing three different distance races (Sprint, Super, and Beast). This included the granddaddy of them all: the Beast in Killington, Vermont. Think of running, hiking, swimming, and carrying stuff up and down one of the steepest mountains in the Northeast. Everyone has their idea of fun ways to spend five-and-a-half hours on a weekend in order to achieve amazing heights.

Back in Chapter 2, we discussed how parents' diets and genetics impact the height of their children. Whether you are considering children or not, hopefully you're agreeable to a healthy diet. I hear from my married friends that I am in good shape *because* I don't have kids. Granted, there is some merit to having additional disposable time; however, just like you can choose to stay active, you can choose to cook healthy or indulge in fast food.

It amazes me how many people still don't understand that physical fitness really does require a combination of exercise and a healthy diet. Even if you aren't into weights, yoga, or other activities, what you eat is absolutely within reach (if not, grab a stool). The fad diets you see may or may not work and could even be dangerous. What *does* work is committing to a plan and making healthy eating a habit. If you've hit the 30-day mark in the past thinking it was the promised land, only to return to your old ways, I'd urge you to consider the research that suggests it takes 66 days to form a habit. At this stage, I'm not even tempted to stop at fast food restaurants. This wasn't always the case. For example, during my NYC advertising days, there were many liquid lunches. Maybe not quite on par with AMC's *Mad Men,* but you get the idea. These days, lunchtime ammo is much more likely to be the Magic Bullet than the other Bulleit (bourbon). Staying active and healthy eating are simply part of my lifestyle. Difficult decisions for me these days are whether to add kale, spinach, or blueberries to my plant-based protein shake (sometimes it's all three). Eating healthy doesn't have to be a major time investment once you've invested the initial cash outlay for healthy ingredients and a few cooking tools. As a two-step cook, I tend to open packages (step one) then empty contents into a bowl or frying pan (step two). Trader Joe's and Whole Foods have tons of options that fit my culinary skills, or lack thereof.

Admittedly I may be a bit obsessive about nutrition these days. I am not a professional athlete, but I love the Jim Rohn quote and believe in the old saying "you are what you eat." What do you suppose world class athletes are consuming to maximize performance? How about the leadership of high-flying tech companies like Amazon, Facebook, and Google? If you see pictures of Zuckerberg, Bezos, or Brin, you'll notice these guys are looking relatively lean and mean. The demands of running three of the most powerful companies in the world require them to take care of themselves. These guys understand that good health allows them to optimize their respective performances. I'm not a nutritionist, but I've read tons of research on the benefits of greens, antioxidants, whole grains, and the like. I'm guessing these tech guys have a similar idea, too. If we've got one body, we might as well take care of it.

Yes, healthy food is more expensive than cheaper, low-quality food. I argue that the added benefits of good food outweigh the alternatives. Can't afford organic? Go with non-genetically modified (non-GMO) food, or find labels that promise no antibiotics have been used on the animals. Free range is also good. Within reason, I find it fun to test different regiments and recently started a Pescatarian diet (similar to a vegetarian diet, but includes seafood). OK, I'll get down off the soap box ... and yes, I left myself wide open for a short joke, so enjoy! Please tip your servers.

Chapter-17

Dating and Social

The dating site OKCupid reports that heights for men on its site are about two inches taller than they are in reality. We know why. This fits nicely with society's height bias and the tendency to stretch the measuring stick when self-reporting. My exaggerated twenty-plus years of self-reporting 5'9" status as a "fact" is just another example of this playing out. If you tell yourself something is the truth for long enough, you really do start to believe it.

In his blog, dating coach Harris O'Malley (who is 5'8") drops knowledge in his piece *5 Dating Tips for Short Men:*[8]

It's not how tall you are; it's how tall people feel you are. There are some people who can fill a room, regardless of how tall they are or aren't.

---

[8] http://www.doctornerdlove.com/5-dating-tips-for-short-men/

They're the ones who stand out in people's memories, who can command attention (and affection) with seeming ease.

One of the best things you can do – especially as a short man – is to develop your sense of presence.

Presence is, simply, your ability to command people's attention. It's the way that you can make people focus on you instead of the distractions that surround them. As I'm always saying: attraction isn't about looks, it's about how you make people feel, and when you can make them feel like they're the only person in the world, you become magnetic.

The best way to develop presence is to be present. OK, before you click the back button in disgust, hear me out. Most of us rarely give our full focus to somebody. We inevitably find our focus divided among the million little things that occupy our attention. But when we feel like someone is giving us their full, undivided attention … it's amazing. They make us feel special. One of the reasons why Tom Cruise is so ridiculously charismatic is because he can make anyone feel like they're the most fascinating person in the world. Simply connecting with them – strong (but not intimidating) eye contact, open and relaxed body language, and actively listening instead of waiting for your turn to talk – is absurdly powerful. When you can build presence, women won't remember you as that short man at the party. They'll remember you as that incredibly charming guy who made them feel like he got them in a way nobody else did.

150

As O'Malley discusses, online dating can be tough for the vertically challenged. I was continually disappointed when running the gauntlet of sites while living in NYC. Was it me? Why is it so difficult to land a date in a city this densely populated?

A 2013 study[9] looked at 50,000 online dating interactions over two months and discovered that the likelihood that a man under 5'9" is contacted by a Manhattan or Bronx woman online is just 1.2 percent. While this particular study did not provide contact rates for men 5'10" and taller, other studies indicate incidence rates range from 10 percent to 30 percent. As previously mentioned, height and power are linked, based on the brain's internal wiring. Money, which can be viewed as a proxy for power, is also desirable when seeking a mate. Consider research from Duke University that uncovers that women will forego height if a man reaches certain levels of income. The brutal truth is that even short women seem to prefer guys who are 5'10" or taller. Research on online dating sites by Duke University professor Dan Ariely has shown that for every inch below 5'10", a man has to earn $40,000 more to be seen as equally appealing to a woman.

Given these findings and height bias, it raises the question: is it acceptable to add two inches to your profile? I have two trains of

---

[9] https://nypost.com/2013/12/08/short-men-dont-stack-up-with-nyc-women/

thought, and one of them goes against the *5 Dating Tips for Short Men* excerpt reviewed a moment ago:

#1) Yes. It's acceptable to add a couple inches, given that everyone else is doing it, including guys who are *already* average height or above. If taller guys are guilty of it and they already have an advantage, it's kind of like Barry Bonds, gifted with amazing baseball talent naturally, doing steroids to get ahead of the competition. Worst case scenario of choosing this approach is you are accused of false advertising. Best case is you help someone overcome their height bias once they learn how great a person you are.

#2) No. If we are going to collectively take a higher road with regards to height bias, then we should take self-reporting more seriously and honestly. Don't exaggerate your height, but know that you could be decreasing your chances by a significant percent by not doing so. And remember, you didn't want to date her anyhow.

Based on my understanding, plus the benefit of research, I'll provide a few additional thoughts on dating. Please note this is based on my views as a heterosexual guy. Our gay and transgender fraternity members may want to consult with others for guidance. With that said, I hope some of what follows is universally applicable.

In my experience, women don't tend to make the first move in the digital domain—or elsewhere. So, don't be afraid to be the one to initiate contact. Also, take time to be thoughtful when sending an intro. Saying "hi" or "what's up?" will almost certainly not be enough to make an impression. If you want to warrant a response, take the time to comment on similar interests or ask about something in particular that caught your eye (I've also found this tactic works great when approaching someone in person). A minute of your time could be the difference between being ignored and going on a date. Think back to the men of action in the Intro and Chapter 3. Each of the highfliers are detail-oriented, and for many, communication is or was a lynchpin for success. Take pride in how you communicate and adopt this mindset to become a man of action, dare I say . . . to get some action.

For additional thoughts and guidance, it may be worth checking out Aziz Ansari's book Modern Dating. While the analysis isn't specifically catering to vertically challenged guys, Ansari is 5'6". Ansari's book provides some best practices that could be helpful. For example, if you're trying to make plans with a girl, be specific about a day and time. Have a couple of places top-of-mind if she says yes. Women appreciate it if a guy has a plan of action.

How about more practical thoughts on making inroads with women in the real world, or "organically" as some would say? Time and time again, you will hear that confidence is sexy. Overcoming doubts we've created, directly or indirectly fueled by society's height bias, can present challenges to our self-confidence. While height is wired into women's minds as desirable, there are other ways to be interesting that will catch a girl's attention. The ability to walk up to a girl and introduce yourself in a social setting is no easy feat. Many women are impressed with the act, even if you aren't super smooth with the delivery. You can make the argument that the less rehearsed you sound, the more authentic and real you will be. Authenticity is a nice differentiator in a sea of sharks.

Or, your approach can be as simple as having good manners. Acts of chivalry do not tend to go unnoticed. In the right setting, manners can be as simple as a thoughtful please or thank you to a barista or server, which should be common sense. Opening a door for a girl can instantly put you on the map as a guy worth getting to know. Hey, open the door for her and the guy she's with—he may be her platonic friend, or she may have a single girlfriend who's looking to meet a quality guy (like you). These things happen every day. Small acts of kindness provide building blocks to being a better person. That by itself is attractive.

If you're looking for a morale-boosting story from yours truly along the lines of *short guy dates tall girl,* here you go: In college I briefly dated a girl who was 6'2". Her friends said she was actually 6'3", giving merit to the fact that height bias can go the other way, as being too tall can also be challenging, especially for females. My girlfriend was from a small town in South Carolina, and I was the guy from New England. I found her attractive, and she was kind of goofy. Note: women with quirky humor apparently dig guys with it as well. We hit it off, and I was amazed to find out I was the first guy to kiss her (we'll leave it here—this isn't *Fifty Shades of Gray*). I learned that guys were extremely intimidated by her height. I was the goofy and vertically challenged guy who had just enough courage to chat her up, even if it meant reaching for the stars, literally and figuratively. She didn't care that I was more than half a foot shorter. We were kids from opposite worlds on a number of levels, height included. It was just one chapter of a fun college experience, but there's your token story. There may be one or two others in my head, but a gentleman doesn't kiss and tell (unless it's content for a self-improvement book). Looking for more recent examples? OK, you win. In the summer of 2017, I dated a girl who was six feet tall. She also happened to be over ten years younger than me and from Canada, but let's not put too many variables out there for consideration. Although these US-Canadian relations fizzled, we are still friends. And no, I did not use height enhancing shoes while dating this girl. Taller women have never been my target, per se. I tend to find myself attracted to females who share an interest in the outdoors or participate in similar activities, as this one did.

As I began writing this book in November 2017, the whole notion of shoe inserts eventually piqued my interest. I went so far as to conduct an experiment to see if the new girl I was pursuing noticed the 3" lift from my shoe inserts. For those of you doing math, these inserts took me to the highly coveted 5'10" status. Unfortunately, my experiment and $10 investment didn't elicit any reaction from her.

Noticing I was somewhat disappointed after I divulged the experiment, she responded, "Maybe that shows you that I like you for you and not your height." Aw shucks, I'm blushing. This may be just one example, but it's safe to say there are other women out there who similarly don't care about height. So quit just thinking about it and ask that girl out. Even if you get turned down, it may dent the ego initially, but it will be a confidence builder in the long haul.

Communicating is an asset in business, and is also valuable in social settings. This year, I travelled to Barcelona for a technology conference hosted by SAP. While most folks at the conference were from the States, I could also carry a conversation in Spanish with locals (Catalan is the other native tongue) when venturing off between sessions or in the evening. In case you're not aware, English is essentially the default language for the world, particularly in business. This means Americans tend to be lazy in learning languages. It pains me to hear Americans poke fun at someone who isn't a native speaker. Let's chalk this up as ignorant. If you want to gain respect from people, including women, when travelling abroad, find the courage to at least try speaking the native tongue. I can almost guarantee they won't make fun of you. You'll immediately separate yourself from the pack. You won't be the vertically challenged guy, but instead the interesting and worldly guy who has the cojones to make an effort to communicate. If your idea of adventure is limited to surfing new channels, consider getting a passport and traveling. Some of the best experiences in my life have occurred while traveling abroad. Give it a try. Austin Powers (Mike Myers) and Jason Bourne will approve. Powers is played by Mike Myers (5'8") and Matt Damon, who plays Jason Bourne, is *allegedly* 5'10". Matt, is that with shoes? We've gotta ask. Our fraternity would gladly welcome you.

Still looking for an edge? Check out *The Game* by Neil Strauss. One page of his playbook actually comes from the almighty peacock. Hey, you wanted more, so stay with me here. To gain the attention of female peacocks, the male peacock flaunts his stuff through a display of his feathers. You've probably seen this action where they fan out their feathers—it's colorful and eye-catching. For our purposes, a fedora with a feather, although an option, would likely be considered overkill. Think of something more subtle. Some guys are into shoes; others like watches. Treat it like an experiment. You may even get a compliment, which leads to conversation. This isn't something I practice regularly, but one recent New Year's Eve I wore a silver bow tie that lit up. It was definitely a conversation starter. Probably not something you'd sport on an average Friday night … but you get the idea. As you build your presence, don't be afraid to combine multiple ideas.

Chapter-18

Appearance

It sounds so simple, but doesn't it make sense to maximize what you've got? How is your posture? If you're like a lot of people (myself included), it may not be quite as good as you think. Poor posture can decrease your height by up to two inches.

Author and health enthusiast Bart Loews (5'7") is part of our fraternity. He dives into the importance of posture:

"35% of your height is accountable to your spine and if you improve or correct your posture that you think is incorrect then it is possible for you to increase your height up to 1 to 2 inches than your present height. Most of the time, people do not realize the importance of correct posture for maximizing height potential and thus they exclude themselves of extra height. Many people look one to two inches shorter than their real height because of their bad or improper postures. You need to take improving your postures seriously if you really want to increase your height. You won't

benefit from height increasing exercises if you don't practice proper posture."

Thank you for the knowledge bombs, Bart. If you want to try see how good, bad, or ugly your posture is, try standing with your heels, butt, and shoulder blades to the wall and tuck your chin. Feels comfortable, right? I log some crazy hours at the computer and find myself increasingly leaning my chin out over my body. This is no bueno. Check YouTube for videos on posture-correcting exercises. One I've embraced daily is a three-minute routine you do twice a day. After I did the first round, I found immediate relief/improvement. All I needed was a wall and the ability to extend my arms outwards at a 45-degree angle.

Find an exercise you like and commit to it. Yoga is also good for helping maintain good posture. In between annual visits with my primary care physician, I "grew" nearly half an inch. This may have been due to being measured in the morning—I believe my previous appointment was in the afternoon. We measure at our tallest first thing in the morning due to forces of gravity. The nurse who measured me even did a double-take as she was surprised at the difference. Just one month into doing posture correcting exercises and seeing results? Wow, maybe I actually will be 5'9" when all is said and done. I am (somewhat) kidding; however, the key takeaway here is that the benefits of proper posture should be noted for maximizing your appearance and confidence, plus your long-term neck and back health.

Try monitoring yourself periodically throughout the day, especially if you are sitting at a desk.

Wayne Gladstone, a columnist in Cracked, brings up pros and cons of being vertically challenged. For the record, he stands 5'6".

Pro: appearing younger than you actually are

"I have no idea why people equate height with age, since most of us stop growing by 18, but they do. When I was 30, people thought I was 22. Yes, I had washboard abs; yes, my skin was smooth and beautiful, like a perfectly crafted Michelangelo sculpture; yes, my hair flowed smoothly with Adonis-like grace, but I don't think that was it. I think it was because I'm short. For some reason, people always think short guys are younger, as if you're still developing."

This is interesting. Depending on your age, you may not want to appear younger. Despite hitting the age of forty, I continue to get asked for my ID when buying alcohol. This is partly due to (self-reported) boyish good looks, but on a serious note, I'd have to agree with Gladstone. Guys, if you're looking for more silver linings to being on the shorter side, a youthful appearance is good, especially as we add years.

Next, Gladstone discusses a setting which most of us would consider to be viewed as a con: *Standing next to tall guys.*

"When a short guy stands next to a freakishly tall guy, he is no longer a short guy. Hell, he's not even a guy anymore. He becomes some sort of halfling. A mythical creature devoid of testosterone or the right to be loved. We have no choice. We just have to avoid it. Watch The Daily Show when my hero, Jon Stewart, has a tall guest. He actually takes a step back to create distance and lets his guest sit before he does. I don't blame him. I do the same thing in real life."

A few thoughts on clothing as it certainly impacts appearance. In business and social settings, style counts. Having lived in major cities such as New York, Los Angeles, and Boston, I've seen a fairly wide range of styles as well as shapes and sizes of people. Guys, pay attention here: if you are short, baggy clothes can suggest that you're even shorter. By all means, I'm an advocate of wearing what's comfortable, but I also like to maximize my frame and appearance. For us sub-five-ten guys who want to maximize what we've got, clothes that fit can work wonders. Suits and sport coats aside, I'm not saying you have to get everything tailored. If you have a thin or slim frame, try to find "slim fit" cut clothes. Full disclosure: one of my fraternity brothers (6'0", 200 lbs) consistently ribbed on me about being a Smurf— in a brotherly way, of course. I still remember a weekend reunion where he pointed at my shirt and asked in front of a group, *"Ulinski, what is that? A boy's medium?!"* Now, it was funny and yes, I embrace working out and being fit, so a form-fitting shirt was on display that day (for the record, it was a slim-fit shirt from Kenneth Cole). However, this gave me the idea the next time I was shopping to actually check out the young men's section. Should you be able to swallow your ego and go with this strategy, the benefits include a wider selection than the men's section and slightly lower prices. The down sides: styles may be a bit too loud for an adult male, and quality could also be on the lower end. For those that don't yet have the "I don't give a crap" attitude that will allow you to shop in the young men's section at T.J. Maxx or Marshalls, it may be helpful to tell yourself that you're simply shopping for a nephew or little bother. Heaven forbid you bump into a buddy or someone else who may judge you. Younger guys reading this will someday understand that caring what others think becomes less important as you get older.

Like me, you may not be satisfied with these shopping options. After all, if there are 60 million guys in the United States under 5"10", wouldn't it make sense that some fashion label had taken note of the market opportunity? After reading a couple of threads (pun intended) on blogs, I hit pay dirt. Founded by Peter Manning in 2012, the Peter Manning NYC clothing line caters to men 5'8" and under. I reached out to Peter to get his thoughts on why virtually every major men's label has a one-size-fits-all mentality about our massive fraternity. His response was, *"No one's complaining, they're going to tailors and settling on ill-fitting clothes . . . it's hard to believe they've ignored this guy, but they have."*

As a consumer, Peter was tired of the lack of clothing options for shorter guys. He decided to take action and launch his company.

163

While the Peter Manning NYC clothing line addresses a big challenge, it operates in a competitive sector. Even the "not-so-tall guy" niche is finally attracting attention. For example, in October 2017, Detroit-based Ash & Erie appeared on Shark Tank and received funding from Mark Cuban. When I asked Manning about where his company wants to be positioned in the space, he stated, "We're not trying to be a leader in men's fashion, but we are trying to be a leader in fit."

If you're interested in more on clothing and style to maximize what you've got, stay with me. It may be common sense for most, but horizontal stripes tend to shorten and "fatten" people—or at least give that illusion. Consider that sometimes wider is better. On the opposite side, vertical stripes are good for lengthening. Belts can also make someone look shorter; however, I often struggle to tuck in a shirt and go without a belt. Call me old school. However, dress pants that have cuffs are a no-no if you want to maximize your height. The same goes for a "break" in the pant leg—it should basically drop straight. See your tailor for details. And for sport coats or suits, the top button of the jacket should be above your navel. Paying attention to these small yet important details about your clothes can only help, not hurt, your standing. I am more of a jeans and t-shirt guy whenever possible, but clothes that are comfortable and look good tend to make me feel good.

Perhaps you are interested in some of these best practices but your funds are limited, you may consider adding just a few slightly more expensive, better-fitting clothes.

If you think clothing is overrated, plenty of women would rather date a guy who's well-dressed than a guy with a nice car. Next time you're out, take a poll. My European friends tell me that it's not uncommon for people to have one *really* nice set of clothes that they wear each and every time they go out on the town. Sounds a bit like a game day uniform.

While clothes can provide a mental boost or give an illusion, boots and shoe inserts can provide an actual lift. If someone asks how tall you are and your immediate follow-up is something to the effect of "is that with or without shoes?", chances are you're part of the less-than-average height club and looking for any help you can get. Most of us in this contingent, especially those who've played sports, have probably stretched our tale of the tape in order to minimize the short label and overcome height bias. Even many top-level professional athletes succumb: While reviewing official draft-day measurements and comparing the numbers to those on their current rosters, I noticed that the latter statistic tends to be an inch or two higher, on par with the OKCupid data.

If you're into exploring new ways to gain an inch or three, elevator shoes or shoe inserts may be worth considering. No one needs to know you're wearing them, and they can add anywhere from one to three inches to your height. For some of you, this seemingly trivial boost may make you feel more confident in social situations. Guys, do be forthcoming if you're hitting the town with your buddies and inform them beforehand. Can you imagine meeting up with one of your pals ... and he's magically three inches taller? If you're going to go this route, enlist your friends' support in advance so as to stay clear of awkward situations when you're out and about. Get them to sign on before any social adventures/experiments, so you can be more relaxed and enjoy the view.

As a market researcher, I had to see what shoe lift options were available. A quick search on Amazon gave me a number of inserts designed precisely for the guy looking to add an inch or three. While boots with heels (i.e. elevator shoes) exist and are straightforward, my $10 investment for some beefy inserts were worth it. Anything for research. The inserts came in three components, adding anywhere from one inch to three inches. Ah yes, using all three would bring me to the promised land of 5'10". The whole endeavor seemed silly, but you don't know what you don't know.

On my first day with inserts, I found them relatively comfortable, but they do require a bit of getting used to as far as your stride and how your foot hits the floor. Watch out for scuffing your feet or tripping. As we know, the taller you are, the harder you fall. Adding the inserts made it so my heel was almost completely exposed, which was awkward and dangerous. If I had to run or do something other than stand or walk, it would have been a disaster. Boots or high-tops would have been a better option than my casual shoes.

You're probably thinking, this is all great, but how was the view up there? The new vantage point was pretty eye-opening, and I'll go so far as to say slightly empowering. Just looking in the mirror was kind of surreal. However, I had to take this show on the road. At the office, it was a bit odd looking directly in the eyes of colleagues who were typically a couple notches up from me. My boss at the time was 6'3" and happened to make a "big guy" comment. This got my attention, but he was simply being playful. Where's the HR manager when you need them? For the record, he and I actually got along well and I felt like he respected me. Not everyone is so fortunate. Between pay gaps and glass ceilings, shorter people can find themselves getting the short end of the stick.

Inserts could be valuable when walking into a situation such as a business negotiation, where you want to feel that extra bit of confidence. Just be careful you don't tip over. If a social setting doesn't require too much moving around, it may be fun to try these in the wild. Just keep in mind that dancing may not be an option, unless the robot is your go-to. Also, the long-term effect inserts may have on walking stride and posture shouldn't be taken lightly. The inserts certainly changed my gait and to a lesser extent, my posture. Keep tabs on each if you decide to conduct your own experiment. On that note, perhaps someone's interested in buying my inserts? I'm Agent 057 and owning it.

As we close this chapter on appearance, you may still have questions. This is a book; fashion is visual. With that in mind, I'd suggest checking out TheModestMan.com for in-depth clothing reviews, trends, and best practices that cater to the "short(er)" guy. It's been a great resource for me, and I had the pleasure of speaking with its founder, Brock McGoff, who is 5'6". When I asked Brock about his mindset about guys like us who are below average height, he said he always thought of us as the underdogs. Great minds think alike. Thank you, Brock.

Chapter-19

Redefining Height

Depending on the setting, height can take on a different meaning. Yes, per Merriam-Webster's dictionary, height has more than one definition. It led me to the title for this book, which makes it a double entendre. For example, height can also be defined as the *summit, apex, or pinnacle.* If you're with me here, you may just find yourself adopting some of these meanings and tailoring them for your profession, hobby, craft, or life ambitions. How high a level can you achieve in the areas where you're passionate? Maybe you'll finally take the plunge into a new area you've been considering? Or maybe you'll take some risks in your current area to continue growing?

While I never ascended to 6'3" or even average height, I am extremely grateful for my health and for being able to participate in a wide range of activities and working on cool projects (including this book) that align with my interests and passions. Was I ever disappointed that I didn't get to dunk or throw a 90-mile-per-hour fastball? Sure. Have I been turned down by women due to my height? Absolutely. Did getting cut from my high school basketball team suck? You bet. However, my abilities and passions pointed me down new paths and adventures, including this book.

If you've read this far, hopefully you'll agree that outside of playing in the NBA (which is still possible, if unlikely), there are plenty of avenues where the only limits are based on your interests, drive, and determination. Things may change for you as you gain new experiences and evolve as a person. My passions and interests ten years ago were much different than they are today.

As Bob Dylan once said, *"People seldom do what they believe in. They do what is convenient, then repent."* Most people don't regret the things they did; rather, they regret the things they *didn't* do. This is why Amazon founder Jeff Bezos views things through his eighty-year-old self when making big decisions.

Today my height has nearly zero impact in my work and play. Nothing holds me back from doing market research, running 5Ks, climbing 4,000-foot mountains in New Hampshire, hablando español, weight-training, ripping guitar chords, playing Star Wars with my nephew, practicing yoga, competing in Spartan Races, and skiing glaciers in Switzerland.

Regardless of height or profession, everyone hits speed bumps. Tough times can be used as learning and growth opportunities. Any entrepreneur will tell you that many times, losing a key client or not getting funded was a character builder or blessing in disguise. Many athletes vividly recall getting axed from a team, only to rise to greatness the next season or in years to come. Even Michael Jordan, considered by many to be the best basketball player of all time, missed the cut in high school. Sometimes just a slight change of course is all that is needed to attain superstar status in your chosen discipline.

If we look at Doug Flutie's career, he went from a solid QB starting in the NFL to a legit superstar in the CFL. Sure, you can use the big fish, small pond analogy if you like. I would argue that Flutie reached even more amazing heights in his career, including happiness, once he let go of his crush on the NFL:

"My first two years in the CFL, all I thought of was getting back to the NFL - it was like 'I'll put my time in up here and go back.' Then I went and signed a nice contract in Calgary and was like, 'Hey, I can make a living up here, this is great football, and I'm having a blast."

~ Doug Flutie

It's up to you to decide how much height bias affects your life. In some ways, the material presented here in this book could be viewed as an investment of time and money. It's up you to deem what's necessary or worth considering. For you slouchers out there, good posture is a minimal investment of a few minutes a day. You could start by monitoring how you sit at your desk. Maybe a one- or two-inch shoe insert is a worthwhile purchase—consider it an extension of my own social experiment. Tell your friends its part of a larger research project, but you're unable to legally disclose any details. You may find that although nobody else notices these steps, you may get a boost of confidence anyway. Have fun with it.

Now I'd like to venture further into an intangible: the mind. A lot of our challenges and obstacles are those we create in our head. Given society's *belief* that tallness equals strength, intelligence, and power—whereas shortness is believed to mean less educated, and in general, less desirable—it's no wonder many of us have created mental barriers. It's up to us, our fraternity of 60 million, to start embracing the opportunities and maximizing what we have, both physically and mentally.

Find your strengths and passion or passions. Sports, business, music, art, public speaking, whatever it is, go for it. It may be a cliché, but you only live once. I'm not saying live with reckless abandon like the YOLO cult suggests, but do what you enjoy, and if anything I've mentioned resonates even a bit, then give it a try. You may even find it's fun to experiment with different tools and tactics. They can be as simple as a frame of mind, stepping up to a microphone, or for you peacocking fans, adding a piece of flare. Otherwise, simply embrace what you've got, like Dustin Pedroia, the self-described mini-badass. And Dustin, if you're reading, can you confirm adding two inches to your roster height? This would make you an even *bigger* mini baddass.

Upon winning Major League Baseball's AL MVP in 2017, the 5'6" Jose Altuve declared:

"That's what I love about baseball, that every single guy can play the game … there's not a rule you have to be six feet tall to play baseball and become a good player."

Let that marinate for a few minutes. The longer you are on this planet, the more you may believe Altuve's statement can extend to other areas. The rules are…there really are no rules. Yes, there are stereotypes and long-standing beliefs that serve as barriers to entry, but many times these barriers are inconsequential compared to the ones we create in our mind. Do you really love a sport or another activity? Do you find yourself enjoying the grind and hard work in perfecting your craft? Are you willing to give up *fill in the blank* to pursue your passions?

As a former advertising guy, I think the following excerpt from a Nike ad circa 1992 with Barry Sanders speaks volumes about his character:

"There's really no time to be afraid. So stop. Try something you've never tried. Risk it. Enter a triathlon. Write a letter to the editor. Demand

a raise. Call winners at the toughest court. Throw away your television. Bicycle across the United States. Try bobsledding. Try anything. Speak out against the designated hitter. Travel to a country where you don't speak the language. Patent something. You have nothing to lose and everything to gain."

Granted, this message was delivered through an ad, but it carries weight if you consider that after losing in the playoffs that year, Barry did indeed try out for the U.S. Olympic Bobsled National Team in Lake Placid, New York. One of the greatest running backs in the NFL gave bobsledding a shot. He was looking for that next thing, that test, that experience to help him grow as a person. Although he didn't make the team, I am confident he would do it again if he had a chance to do it all over again.

I love to write about a wide range of topics and sift through data. The combination of these passions makes me a great fit for working in market research. My height doesn't prevent me from pursuing career opportunities as an author or market researcher. Similarly, my free time consists of outdoor recreation, endurance and athletic events, plus traveling the world.

And if you wince at the thought of self-improvement, remember that it's a broad category. Check out the aforementioned Tim Ferriss. His books and podcasts are inspiring and educational. Not to say you should limit yourself to guidance from those who are part of our fraternity. I certainly don't. However, I do think it's valuable knowing, at a minimum, these stars have viewed the world from similar vantage points.

In his own words, Ferriss says, *"I was really small and got my ass kicked mercilessly up until about sixth grade. So I wouldn't go out to the playground."*[44] His mom would push him into wrestling, a sport he competed in through high school. He credits confidence gained on the mat for his quest for knowledge and experiments in life, which are the core tenets of his books and podcasts. Opportunities in what I'll call the knowledge economy are enormous today, and height has no bearing on how high you can go. If you aren't familiar with him, I'd recommend listening to one of Ferriss's podcasts.

If you're looking for a tool to help get you moving, Mel Robbins's *5 Second Rule* spurred me on countless times. Her *Stop Screwing Yourself* TED talk is on YouTube and provides a glimpse at her philosophy. Mel introduces the 5-second rule near the end of her talk; she later produced an audio book specifically on this tool. If fear is holding you back, you may want to check out Brené Brown's book, *The Power of Vulnerability: Teachings on Authenticity, Connection & Courage.* It helped galvanize my idea of putting my thoughts and experiences on display. In this work and her subsequent book, *Daring Greatly,* Brown examines Theodore Roosevelt's speech, popularly known as *"The Man in the Arena."* By default, Mel and Brené aren't part of our fraternity, but if you're trying to break out of a rut or you're putting yourself on a stage where others may judge you, reading

Roosevelt's speech and Brené's book might give you courage and solace.

As Roosevelt's famous speech suggests, those of us who are willing to take action may be entering an arena of some kind. Your arena could be an audience of one, a small group, or the entire world. If you are ready and willing, be prepared for criticism; however, as our sixth president proclaimed:

"It is not the critic who counts; not the man who points out how the strong man stumbles or where the doer of deeds could have done them better. The credit belongs to the man who is actually in the arena, whose face is marred by dust and sweat and blood; who strives valiantly; who errs, who comes short again and again, because there is no effort without error and shortcoming; but who does actually strive to do the deeds; who knows great enthusiasms, the great devotions; who spends himself in a worthy cause; who at the best knows in the end the triumph of high achievement, and who at the worst, if he fails, at least fails while daring greatly, so that his place shall never be with those cold and timid souls who neither know victory nor defeat."[45]

By publishing a book, I put myself in the arena for others to judge. My writing style and sense of humor have been described as quirky. Added bonus? Height is a sensitive subject. Concerned with offending readers, I did extensive survey work on Facebook and PickFu to identify the best title and subtitle. I found that the word *short* is considered demeaning to some people, while the term *vertically challenged* can also be a lightning rod. I learned there is no perfect way to write a book, just like there is no perfect way to describe men who are below average height. At least I can say I'm walking the walk, usually with a smile on my face.

A couple of my buddies provided valuable perspectives on achieving things in the face of height bias:

"My perspective has always been that my height falls under the category of things I have zero control over. Since it is completely out of my hands, I don't [think about height] as a hindrance for me . . . I am an internal locus of control kind of guy, I don't allow myself to have circumstances happen to me, I believe there is always something I can do to influence a situation."

~ Rob, 5'7", MBA, Project Owner, Fortune 50 Company

"As far as I'm concerned, it's always been other peoples' hang up, not mine. Even when I was a much younger man, self-assurance carried me through and made it easier for me to do whatever I wanted to do successfully."

~ Glenn, 5'5", History Ph.D

Hopefully these stories, studies, and memoirs have been interesting and inspiring. There are tremendous opportunities in life, but we have to own our life and take action. Major hurdles and setbacks will happen to us regardless of our height. Take action and don't be afraid to try new things. Enter the arena. Focus on what you can control. Push past those false cognitive biases around height so you can continue to grow and achieve amazing things. If you've learned anything from this book, you should now realize that height is not a precursor for social status or how high you can go in life. The key ingredient is *action*.

As a follow-up to this book, I'm developing a podcast that will provide deeper dives into these topics, plus explore other ideas. I'll interview guys in our fraternity who are reaching amazing heights, including some mentioned in this book. Perhaps you or someone you know has a story to share? If so, I'd love to hear your thoughts and experiences. By taking notes on strategies and tools for success, we can collectively stand tall as we achieve our goals in life. You can connect with me on social media and visit AmazingHeights.blog to receive updates.

If you liked Amazing Heights and feel you've benefited from reading it, I hope you'll share a review on Amazon. Thank you for reading. Keep standing tall.

Author Bio

Seth Ulinski resides in Dover, NH. He graduated from Clemson University, South Carolina, with a B.A. in Spanish and International Trade. While attending Clemson, Seth became a member of Pi Kappa Phi Fraternity. At 5'7", he is also a member of the short guy fraternity.

Since he was a kid, Seth has been fascinated with sports. Seth played basketball, baseball, and football until a car accident in his sophomore year of high school. Multiple surgeries and a long recovery process gave him a stronger appreciation for seatbelts and good health. As an adult, Seth was diagnosed with autoimmune disorders, requiring thyroid and eye surgery. While educating himself on how to manage these life-altering events, Seth realized the value of self-care. Today, he's grateful for these setbacks, drawing from them as part of his wider self-improvement work.

His professional background includes two decades of work in digital advertising and market research. As a salesman, Seth experienced the ad industry's transition from *Mad Men* to math men. As an IT analyst, he authored reports analyzing business trends of the IT landscape.

Seth is a member of SIX03 Endurance, Portsmouth Toastmasters, and the Seacoast Ski Club. When he isn't training for a race, skiing, or practicing his next speech, Seth enjoys spending time with family and friends.

In addition to being vertically challenged, some may say Seth is directionally challenged. He insists he isn't lost but prefers the scenic view and the adventure that comes with it.

Sources

1. Heuristics in Judgment and Decision-making. Accessed January 2018
    https://en.wikipedia.org/wiki/Heuristics_in_judgment_and_decision-making.

2. Growing Taller. December 2011.
    https://talk.collegeconfidential.com/parent-cafe/1261074-growing-taller.html

3. Venton, Danielle. "Power Postures Can Make You Feel More Powerful." *Wired.* June 03, 2017.
    https://www.wired.com/2012/05/st-cuddy/

4. "Why You Shrink As You Age." July 2015.
    http://www.berkeleywellness.com/self-care/preventive-care/article/why-you-shrink-you-age.

5. List of Average Human Height Worldwide. Accessed December 2017.

https://en.wikipedia.org/wiki/List_of_average_human_height_worldwide.

6.   Lai CQ. How much of human height is genetic and how much is due to nutrition? *Scientific American,* Questions and Comments, 2006. Dec. 11.

7.   Viking Age. Accessed November 2017. https://en.wikipedia.org/wiki/Viking_Age.

8.   Bolotoff, Paul V., and Greg Nichols. "Why Were the Vikings so Much Taller than Europeans of the Same Era?" Accessed February 2018. https://www.quora.com/Why-were-the-Vikings-so-much-taller-than-Europeans-of-the-same-era

9.   Scandinavia. Accessed February 2018. https://en.wikipedia.org/wiki/Scandinavia.

10. Loewens, Stanley C. "Short Man Syndrome Explained." HealthGuidance.org. Accessed December 2017. http://www.healthguidance.org/entry/15851/1/Short-Man-Syndrome-Explained.html.

11. Van Schneider, Tobias. "If You Want It, You Might Get It. The Reticular Activating System Explained." June 2017. https://medium.com/desk-of-van-schneider/if-you-want-it-you-might-get-it-the-reticular-activating-system-explained-761b6ac14e53.

12. Cialdini, Robert B. *Influence: The Psychology of Persuasion.* New York, NY: Collins.

13. Keller, Gary, and Jay Papasan. *The One Thing: The Surprisingly Simple Truth behind Extraordinary Results.* Austin, TX: Bard Press, 2013.

14. *A Football Life: Barry Sanders.* Directed by Nick Mascolo and Paul Manusky. United States: NFL Films, 2013. DVD.

15. Robinson, Nate, and Jon Finkel. *Heart over Height.* Raleigh, NC: Lulu Publishing Services, 2014.

16. McGillivray, David J., and Linda Glass. Fechter. *The Last Pick: The Boston Marathon Race Directors Road to Success.* Emmaus, PA: Rodale, 2006.

17. Robson, David. "Future – Tall vs Short: Which Is It Better to Be?" BBC. September 29, 2015. http://www.bbc.com/future/story/20150928-tall-vs-small-which-is-it-better-to-be.

18. National Baseball Hall of Fame. Accessed December 2017. https://baseballhall.org/hall-of-famers/keeler-willie

19. Major League Baseball Players Alumni Association. Accessed December 2017. https://en.wikipedia.org/wiki/Major_League_Baseball_Players_Alumni_Association

20. Miller, Scott. "Once Ignored by MLB, 5'6" Superstar Jose Altuve May Now Be Its MVP." Bleacher Report. October 2017. http://bleacherreport.com/articles/2735785-once-ignored-by-mlb-56-superstar-jose-altuve-may-now-be-its-mvp.

21. *Baseball America's Ultimate Draft Book.* Durham, NC: Baseball America, 2016. https://baseballamerica.myshopify.com/products/ultimate-draft-book.

22. "Brad Marchand Named Most Stylish Bostonian." The Boston Globe. September 2011. http://thesportsdaily.com/days-of-yorr/brad-marchand-named-most-stylish-bostonian/.

23. "Erik Karlsson, Connor McDavid, Auston Matthews, Johnny Gaudreau Thrill like No Others." ESPN.com. November 2017. http://www.espn.com/nhl/story/_/id/21271565/nhl-most-exciting-superstar-player-watch.

24. Cotsonika, Nicholas J. "Cam Atkinson Playing above His Height." NHL.com. January 2017. https://www.nhl.com/news/columbus-blue-jackets-cam-atkinson-letting-skill-define-game/c-285603020.

25. Murray, Caitlin. "The 50 Highest-paid MLS Players for 2017." Fox Sports. April 2017. https://www.foxsports.com/soccer/gallery/mls-player-salaries-highest-paid-most-expensive-designated-players-042517.

26. "Gene Sarazen." Wikipedia. Accessed January 2018.
    https://en.wikipedia.org/wiki/Gene_Sarazen.

27. "Gary Player." Wikipedia. Accessed January 2018.
    https://en.wikipedia.org/wiki/Gary_Player.

28. 28. Rude, Jeff. "Smallest Player Kruger Swings Big Stick."
    Golfweek.com. March 2012.
    http://golfweek.com/2012/03/10/rude-krugers-game-rise-2012/.

29. Gladwell, Malcolm. *Blink: The Power of Thinking without Thinking.* New York: Back Bay Books, 2013.

30. Warrillow, John. "Why Shorter People Make Better
    Entrepreneurs." Inc.com. Accessed December 2017.
    https://www.inc.com/john-warrillow/the-surprising-role-height-plays-in-your-potential-as-a-leader.html.

31. Judge, Timothy A., PhD, and Daniel M. Cable, PhD.
    "Standing Tall Pays Off." Journal of Applied Psychology vol.
    89, no. 3.

32. Persico, Nicola, Andrew Postlewaite, and Dan Silverman. "The
    Effect of Adolescent Experience on Labor Market Outcomes:
    The Case of Height." Journal of Political Economy 112, no. 5
    (2004).

33. "Jeff Bezos." Wikipedia. Accessed December 2017. https://en.wikipedia.org/wiki/Jeff_Bezos#Early_life_and_education.

34. Constine, Josh. "Jeff Bezos' Guide to Life." TechCrunch. November 07, 2017. https://techcrunch.com/2017/11/05/jeff-bezos-guide-to-life/.

35. "Fire Phone." Wikipedia. Accessed January 2018. https://en.wikipedia.org/wiki/Fire_Phone.

36. Vargas, Jose Antonio. "The Face of Facebook." The New Yorker. June 2017. https://www.newyorker.com/magazine/2010/09/20/the-face-of-facebook.

37. "Sergey Brin." Wikipedia. Accessed December 2017. https://en.wikipedia.org/wiki/Sergey_Brin.

38. "Jack Welch." Wikipedia. Accessed January 2018. https://en.wikipedia.org/wiki/Jack_Welch.

39. "James Madison." Biography.com. April 28, 2017. https://www.biography.com/people/james-madison-9394965.

40. Kooper, Al. "Bob Dylan." Encyclopedia Britannica. February 01, 2018. https://www.britannica.com/biography/Bob-Dylan-American-musician.

41. "Kevin Hart." Wikipedia. Accessed January 2018. https://en.wikipedia.org/wiki/Kevin_Hart.

42. Snowden, Jonathan. "Floyd Mayweather: How His Family's History of Violence Has Shaped Money May." Bleacher Report. April 2017. http://bleacherreport.com/articles/1627330-floyd-mayweather-how-his-familys-history-of-violence-has-shaped-money-may.

43. Croston, Glenn, PhD. "The Thing We Fear More Than Death." Psychology Today. November 2012. https://www.psychologytoday.com/us/blog/the-real-story-risk/201211/the-thing-we-fear-more-death.

44. Richards, Daniel. "'The 4-Hour Workweek' Author Tim Ferriss Reveals What He's Learned after a Difficult Year of Introspection, and How He Built a Passionate Fanbase of Millions." Business Insider. November 18, 2017. http://www.businessinsider.com/tim-ferriss-explains-how-he-built-a-fanbase-of-millions-2017-11.

45. "The Man in the Arena." Theodore Roosevelt Center – Man in the Arena. Accessed March 2018. https://bit.ly/2GFYCfW.

28821140R00113

Made in the USA
Middletown, DE
21 December 2018